A powerful examination of the biblical, linguistic, historical, and archaeological evidence affirming that the creation days of Genesis were nothing but real and literal days. If you think that God worked through evolution, read this book and be challenged. If you believe that God created in a literal six days, read this book and be strengthened.

—**Joseph Farah**, CEO, WorldNetDaily.com Inc.

The modern age seeks to convince us that our world is very old, an idea which can only be accounted for by evolution. Douglas Hamp, however, makes a convincing case that the world was created in six literal days. He utilizes his mastery of the Hebrew language to give insight into the conflict between those holding old earth and young earth views.

Douglas uses quotes from writers of the Early Church Period, both Jewish and Christian, to show their common belief in a six-day creation. He also deals with the ever-present "dinosaur question," presenting evidence that both men and dinosaurs were co-existent. For me, this book was a faith-strengthener in the power of God as Creator.

—**Carl Westerlund** Th.M, Director, Calvary Chapel Costa Mesa School of Ministry and Graduate School

Bookstores are flooded with treatises on creation/evolution apologetics, most being compendia from a common knowledge base, written stylistically by authors of various persuasions. Inductive Darwinian support suffers from lack of substantive fossil records. Familiar lines in the sand are drawn, although with scant new evidence since this history unfolded from the beginning of time. Douglas Hamp's knowledge of the Bible, Theology, and Languages fuels his refreshing and unique deductive approach toward examining results derived through literal interpretation. The ideas of Theistic Evolution cropping up in many circles are convincingly debunked, with new insights into the biblical support and meaning of a six-ordinary-day creation. Issues derived from such a "young earth" result are explained using some of the more recent findings throughout the world.

—**Dr. Stan Sholar**, Retired Aerospace Scientist

Within the past one hundred years we can look back on "scientific absolutes" that no longer are regarded as functional truths. Therefore, we should not be in a hurry to change a simple reading of Scripture based on annual changes within the scientific community! God's Word should be held to be more definite and unchanging simply because it reflects Him as the One who never changes.

Doug has approached the question of whether the first six days of creation were literal or figurative through meticulous research yet with a fluid and easily understood style. Read this book; make your decisions. "It is required of stewards that one be found trustworthy" (1 Corinthians 4:2).

—**Dr. Bill Spear**, Director, Mountain Ministries, Dillon, Colorado

It's wonderful to have an easy-to-read yet well-researched book that demonstrates that a sound reading of Genesis chapter 1 demands a literal, six-day creation week. If you've ever asked yourself whether the first six creation days were real days, or whether it even matters, this book by pastor and educator Douglas Hamp is for you.

—**Ken Ham**, Founder and President, Answers in Genesis and the Creation Museum

THE FIRST SIX DAYS

Confronting the God-Plus-Evolution Myth

Douglas Hamp

The First Six Days
Confronting the God-Plus-Evolution Myth

Copyright © 2008 by Douglas Hamp

Published by Yoel Press
Santa Ana, CA

Cover by Neil Godding

Front cover picture courtesy of www.hubblesite.org

First printing September 2007
Second printing February 2008

Library of Congress Number: 2007933437

ISBN 10: 1-59751-029-7
ISBN 13: 978-1-59751-029-5

Printed in the United States of America.

www.thefirstsixdays.com

Foreword

The theories of uniformitarianism and evolution proposed in the early 1800s, with their need of vast ages of time, challenged the commonly accepted literal, six-day creation of Genesis. Many pastors and theologians, overwhelmed by the apparently indisputable evidence, therefore sought ways to reconcile the two whereby the needed time could fit into the biblical creation.

Over the last several decades the creationist movement has made great strides forward toward the goal of demonstrating that the pro-evolution evidence is full of many holes. In fact, thanks to the diligence of many researchers, the scientific evidence in favor of a biblical creation is gaining constantly. However, the accepted belief of evolution is not easily shaken. Consequently many yet hold to a compromised position asserting that the Bible teaches that God created via evolution and that the days of creation are long day-ages.

Douglas Hamp's work, *The First Six Days*, is a much-needed contribution to settle the question of days or ages. As a Hebrew language specialist trained at the Hebrew University of Jerusalem, he demonstrates convincingly from the pages of Scripture that the days of the Genesis creation account are literal days. He also carefully clarifies some misrepresentations of what *day* means in Hebrew. This is followed up by a stimulating review of the literal, six-day position held by ancient Jewish and Christian interpreters as well as archaeological corroboration of the biblical record.

I recommend this work without reservation, and pray it has a long and fruitful ministry. It makes a real contribution to a pastor's library, and adds power to any Bible teacher's or student's message. The evangelical church badly needs it.

—Dr. John Morris, President, Institute of Creation Research

Contents

List of Pictures

Acknowledgments

I would like to thank the many people that helped to transform the early drafts of this book into a more polished work. Many thanks to Norm Robinson, Jim Pamplin, Brian Harmon, Dr. Bill Gallagher, and Dr. Randall Buth for your thoughts and suggestions on how to improve certain arguments. Thank you Steve Colmer for your detailed and critical eye that helped me to tighten up and to strengthen my case. Thanks David Moo for proofing the book. Thank you very much Dr. Stan Sholar for your critique and important clarifications of the scientific topics discussed in this book. Thank you David Wright and the staff at Answers in Genesis for your help. Thank you Dr. John Morris for writing the foreword to the book. Special thanks to Neil and Romy Godding for the cover and the layout work. Lastly, I would like to thank my beautiful wife for all of her encouragement and support as I wrote this book and also for the many hours of proofing and editing. Thanks for encouraging me to sleep once in a while.

To my sweet daughter, Eliana,
"My God Answered," and to my dear son,
Benjamin, "Son of My Right Hand"

Preface

I have endeavored to write concerning the six days of creation since there is so much confusion concerning them. The evolutionary model has become so widespread and predominant in our society that to believe in the literal reading of the Bible has become extremely unfashionable, certainly for those who do not believe in its message but even for those professing to believe in its authority.

I have written this book not to debunk every argument in favor of evolution, but in order to strengthen your faith in God's Word—that it is true and accurate in all that it says. It does not matter if we are dealing with what some call religious truths or scientific truths. God's Word is sure.

You will notice that my starting assumptions are that God exists and that the Bible is His Word to us and furthermore that the inspiration of the thoughts and very words of the Bible originated with God. Hopefully, you will consider the case that is put forth in this book and will see that God is big enough to create the heavens and the earth in six literal days and be assured that His Word is without error whatsoever. Additionally, it is my desire to show that we do not need to read between the lines of the biblical creation account; God declared that He created in six days.

> For in six days the LORD made the heavens and the earth, the sea, and all that is in them, and rested the seventh day (Exodus 20:11).

Introduction

> Many of the beloved stories found in the Bible—the Creation, Adam and Eve, Noah and the ark—convey timeless truths about God, human beings, and the proper relationship between Creator and creation [...] Religious truth is of a different order from scientific truth. Its purpose is not to convey scientific information but to transform hearts.[1]

This excerpt, from the Clergy Letter Project, encapsulates the sentiment of many people when it comes to the areas of the Bible that touch upon areas of science. If natural (atheistic) science claims something, then the Bible must necessarily take a backseat to it. The purpose of this book is to expose the faulty reasoning of the above statement. We will see from internal evidence of the Bible itself, from external evidence—what others thought about it—and also from some evidence that contradicts the evolutionary paradigm that the biblical creation account is accurate and true. It is not just a beloved story that teaches us religious truth but is true in all that it says.

The question of the origin of the universe is one that most of us will contemplate some time in life, for in it are contained the other big questions in life: Where did this world, solar system, galaxy, and universe come from? How did we all end up here on this planet called earth? Once we understand our origins, we will also yearn to know who we are. Do we have a purpose on this planet? Or is our existence just random and without meaning; and once we die, is that the end or is there life after death? There are essentially two answers, generally speaking: one answer posits that we, all living beings and the entire universe, are the results of many fortuitous chance[2] occurrences. Going back far enough, we arrive at a time or point or singularity, as it were, when all that is was contained in a dot[3], no bigger than one on this page, which then exploded without any outside influence. And from that explosion were formed stars, galaxies, planets, and even space itself. Then life spontaneously generated and evolved over billions of years until finally you and I came along.[4] The other view states that God created all that is by design and intent and that the history of that creation can be found in the pages of the Bible, primarily in the first two chapters of the book of Genesis.

Ironically, the latter view has split in reaction to the first. The question of our study is essentially: did God create in a literal six days (plus the day He rested), as a simple reading of Genesis would suggest, or did God in fact work through the process of evolution over a period of some fifteen billion years? This split in understanding has unfortunately turned into a debate where there are very sincere people on both sides of the issue. I have a friend who believes that God worked through the process of evolution and thus, rather than believing that each of the days described in Genesis refers to a literal day of 24-hours, or one revolution of the earth about its axis, he is convinced that those were long periods of time during which the slow process of evolution was being directed by God. He and I both love God and believe that the Bible is God's revelation to mankind even though we diametrically disagree on this point.

The Goal of Our Study

The question of how long God took to create all that exists undoubtedly stands at the heart of the creationism debate and hence the issue at hand is whether the biblical creation took place over a period of approximately fifteen billion years or just six days. Since there are people who love God on both sides of this issue, we will not judge their devotion to God, but simply examine the Bible and supporting texts to come to the best possible understanding of just how long it took God to create all that is. Of course the question arises: couldn't God have created the universe by way of evolution? Couldn't He have used the slow physical changes as described in evolution to finally get to us and the world as we know it? Obviously, the answer is yes! God could have, but the ultimate question before us is this: did He? Does the Bible actually teach that He created over billions of years? We seek no other matter: did God, as recorded in the Bible, create all that exists in six literal days thousands of years ago? Or did God create over six day-ages in which billions of years passed?

There is a plethora of excellent books and articles written on the subject of the science of the Bible's creation account. Many publications in the fields of physics, geology, biology, chemistry, mathematics, and even law have superbly demonstrated that the Bible's cosmology is not only plausible, but is even a better model of origins than evolution from a strictly scientific point of view. The goal of this book is not to prove the Bible right and evolution wrong from a *scientific* point of view. As I am not a scientist, I encourage the reader to examine the recommended resources and bibliography for a more thorough investigation of the scientific data.

Our investigation will primarily focus on examining supporting biblical texts to observe what the original languages and grammar yield. We will also focus on what ancient Jewish and Christian interpreters believed the Bible to say regarding how long those six days were. The main focus of this book is to demonstrate that six days have always been understood to be real and literal days.

In later chapters, however, we will very briefly consider a few of the hardest questions facing the Bible's teaching of a young earth such as the existence of dinosaurs, the time needed for light that is billions of light years away to arrive to earth in only six-earth days, radioisotope dating of rocks, and how long the Grand Canyon took to form. By doing so, we will test the claim of those who say that the creation account is a religious truth and not scientific truth. If the truth is that God created in six literal days only several thousand years ago, then we expect to see three criteria fulfilled:

1. According to the Bible, the creation days were normal and literal days

2. The overwhelming majority of ancient Jewish and Christian interpreters believed the days were literal and hence thought that the earth was young

3. Archaeological confirmation of biblical account

If we are going to claim that the Bible is, in fact, God's revelation to mankind, then we must be open to letting it guide us to certain conclusions whether those agree with the evolutionary model or not.

1-The Importance of Genesis

Christianity has fought, still fights, and will continue to fight science to the desperate end over evolution, because evolution destroys utterly and finally the very reason Jesus' earthly life was supposedly made necessary. **Destroy Adam and Eve and the original sin, and in the rubble you will find the sorry remains of the Son of God.** If Jesus was not the redeemer who died for our sins, and this is what evolution means, then Christianity is nothing (R. Bozarth 1979: 30, "The Meaning of Evolution," *American Atheist Magazine*, emphasis mine).

God's Word Is Above His Name

Does it really matter what one believes about God's creation? Whether we believe in a literal view of Genesis or that God used evolution; who really cares? There are many reasons that deem this question to be extremely important. First of all, the psalmist declares that "I will worship toward Your holy temple, and praise Your name for Your lovingkindness and Your truth; for **You have magnified Your word above all Your name**" (Psalm 138:2, emphasis mine). God's has magnified His Word (the Bible[5]) above His name. In Isaiah 40:8 we read, "The grass withers, the flower fades, but the word of our God stands forever." Thus, God is very concerned about the reputation of His Word. And if the Bible is from God, then, logically, it should be accurate and faithful in all that it says. Consequently, we read that "Every word of God is pure; He is a shield to those who put their trust in Him. Do not add to His words, lest He rebuke you, and you be found a liar" (Proverbs 30:5–6). We want to neither add to nor subtract from His words since no true follower of God wants to be found a liar by God. It follows then that six literal days or fifteen billion years of creation are two radically different claims. These are so dissimilar to one another that it certainly could be asserted as adding to or subtracting from His words, depending which is in fact correct.

Genesis Is Foundational

Secondly, Genesis chapters 1–11 are the foundation of our worldview. Where we start often determines where we end up. If we interpret those six days to mean simply six days, then we have an easy path for the remainder of the Bible—what it says is what it means. However, if we start down the path that the Scriptures do not say what they actually mean—that there is a buried allegorical meaning that must be mined out of them to truly get to the real meaning, then we will find ourselves not really ever absolutely sure what the Bible means. Since looking for the underlying meaning so much depends on the cleverness of the interpreter rather than on the evidence of archeology, history, biblical grammar, philology, and comparative linguistics, the interpretation becomes very subjective and fuzzy. If the Bible cannot be trusted regarding our origin, how can we trust it regarding our destiny? Jesus even asks the pointed question: "If I have told you earthly things and you do not believe, how will you believe if I tell you heavenly things?" (John 3:12).

If *six days* really means something else, then how do we know that Jesus' statement "no one comes to the Father, but by Me" (John 14:6) doesn't also mean something else? Or how do we know that "he who believes in Me, though he may die, shall live" (John 11:25) doesn't mean something different? If Genesis, the foundation of our origin, where God created man and man disobeyed God and fell, is not accurate or trustworthy, then how do we know that anything else in Scripture truly is? How then do we know that the promises of heaven are true?

The Origin of Marriage

Consider some of the foundational teachings that originate in those first eleven chapters of Genesis. The first description of marriage is found in Genesis 2:24, "Therefore a man shall leave his father and mother and be joined to his wife, and they shall become one flesh." If Adam and Eve were not really our first parents and God didn't really form them as stated in Genesis, then do we really become one flesh? We are left without a clear precedent for marriage. Jesus certainly invoked the first marriage account as a defense against those trying to justify divorce. "And Jesus answered and said to them, '... Because of the hardness of your heart He wrote you this precept. But from the beginning of the creation, God made them male and female'" (Mark 10:5–8). He then added, "so then they are no longer two, but one flesh." The fact that Jesus said "from the beginning ..." proves (if we take Him literally) that He clearly claimed Adam and Eve to have been created in the beginning, not billions of years later as predicated by evolution.

The Origin of Sin and Death

Genesis chapter 3 offers us an insider's view into how sin, death, and suffering came into the world as a result of the disobedience of Adam and Eve (whom Jesus stated were created in the beginning) to God's commandment. If we spiritualize this chapter of the Bible, then what is the historical foundation of our sin-filled world? How do we account for death if Adam and Eve were merely allegorical or symbolic figures who never actually walked this earth and disobeyed their Maker? However, if we use the simple method of literal interpretation, then understanding becomes very easy. Understanding Genesis chapter 3 literally seems to be what Paul did in Romans:

> Therefore, just as through one man sin entered the world, and death through sin, and thus death spread to all men, because all sinned ... nevertheless death reigned from Adam to Moses, even over those who had not sinned according to the likeness of the transgression of Adam, who is a type of Him who was to come (Romans 5:12–14).

Paul states that Adam sinned and so through him, one man, sin spread to all. He also mentions that Adam is a type of Him who was to come. By saying that Adam is a type in no way suggests that Adam was not a real person; rather Adam was the first of a kind, that is (sinful) humanity, and so too Jesus was the first of a kind (humanity holy and without sin). In verse 17 Paul says, "For if by the one man's offense death reigned through the one, much more those who receive abundance of grace and of the gift of righteousness will reign in life through the One, Jesus Christ." Because Paul contrasts Adam with Jesus and since he unquestionably believed Jesus to be a real, historical person, then we can safely conclude that Paul also believed Adam to be a real, historical person.

The Promise of the Redeemer

The importance of the book of Genesis as being a trustworthy and true account of historical and actual events is hopefully evident. Not only does it contain the true history of man's fall, but also the promise of the coming Redeemer. In Genesis 3:15 God promised that someday, one of Eve's offspring would come and make right and annul the effects of their disobedience. "And I will put enmity between you [the Serpent] and the woman, and between your seed and her Seed; He shall bruise your head, and you shall bruise His heel." Ancient Jewish interpretation[6] of this verse likewise understands it to be a promise of the coming Messiah and His remedy for man. To dismiss the creation and fall of man as figurative and not literal is to undermine the very heart of the Bible's message of the coming Redeemer.

2-Evolution Plus God

Evolution plus God is the position that many people have taken when it comes to the first six days of creation. They accept the Bible as God's divine book yet also accept the many facets of evolution as indisputable fact and are forced to squeeze the needed evolutionary time into the pages of the Bible. Before looking at the evolution plus God theories, however, let us first consider what exactly evolution is.

What Is Evolution?

Evolution in its most basic sense is *any process of formation or growth; development*, derived from the Latin meaning *unrolling*, according to *Random House Dictionary* (2006). There are many things that evolve, so to speak, in our world. All that we mean, however, is that there is a slow, gradual change occurring in different facets of life. Let us consider a few examples.

The Changes in Language and Culture

We can speak of the slow progression of the English language as an example of evolution. The English of today is clearly not the same as that of Shakespeare's day. They are both English, but many things have changed radically so that words and expressions of his day have a completely different meaning today. The change in language is something that happens slowly and in small increments, but we can all agree that it happens. Consider how it is that we use different expressions than our parents did and our kids use different words and expressions than we do.

Cultures are also going through a process of change or evolution as well. The culture of America is without doubt different today than it was fifty years ago. Things that were unacceptable back then are sometimes considered normal by today's standards. In both of these examples, however, we are using the word *evolution* as a description of the slow change that is taking place and as such, the concept is completely acceptable. After all, these changes are **observed** linguistically and culturally by experts in the respective fields and simply by the general public. In other words, we can easily document and conclusively prove that those changes have actually occurred because the starting point is only fifty years ago and not fifteen billion or even six thousand years ago.

From Natural Selection to Molecules-to-Man Evolution to Abiogenesis

Using the word *evolution* to describe the slow, steady changes that we undoubtedly witness in languages and cultures is indeed a correct use of the term. If that were the only way that it was used then there would be no problem whatsoever. However, the reality is that *evolution* has been given a new role and meaning; it is used to describe the entire progression of the universe starting with the Big Bang until the present day. The different phases of evolution include: particulate, galactic, stellar, planetary, chemical, biological, and cultural.[7] Biological evolution purports to explain how life started from non-life (properly called abiogenesis) and then how those single-celled organisms eventually turned into you and me. Douglas Futuyma, a foremost expert in biological evolution, notes,

> "In the broadest sense, evolution is merely change, and so is all-pervasive; galaxies, languages, and political systems all evolve. Biological evolution ... is change in the properties of populations of organisms

that transcend the lifetime of a single individual. ... Biological evolution may be slight or substantial; it embraces everything from slight changes in the proportion of different alleles within a population (such as those determining blood types) to the successive alterations that led from the earliest protoorganism to snails, bees, giraffes, and dandelions" (Futuyma 1986).

The above definition is rather misleading, however. Dr. Futuyma should define for us the three different concepts that he is dealing with under the broad category of biological evolution, which are: Natural Selection (adaptation to an environment), molecules-to-man evolution (change in kind, e.g. reptile to bird), and abiogenesis (a nonliving piece of rock to a living single-celled organism). Neither the Bible nor literal six-day creationists are in any way against the concept of Natural Selection, which was actually first introduced by a creationist Edward Blythe. Changes in species populations, by adapting to their environment, have in fact been witnessed to occur.

Charles Darwin correctly noted that the beaks of the finches on the Galapagos Islands changed according to the climatic conditions. He called this evolution. From there he postulated his theory that these small changes, given enough time, could account for all of the living creatures on earth. Darwin failed to note, however, that the finches were still finches. They never turned into something else other than finches. Darwin observed the species' ability to adapt to its surrounding (which is easily ascribed to an amazing Creator) and from there made the leap of faith that with the magical element of time, one creature will turn into another.

According to Its Kind

The belief in molecules-to-man evolution—that single-celled organisms turned into more complex creatures, which turned into something else, all the way to you and me—is what stands in direct conflict with the Bible and specifically the six days of creation. Genesis 1:24 specifically states that on the fifth day, "Then God said, 'Let the earth bring forth the living creature according to its kind [מין min]: cattle and creeping thing and beast of the earth, each according to its kind'; and it was so." This verse acts as an insurmountable obstacle to those who would try to bridge (macro)evolution and the Bible. God's words cannot be misconstrued here. He plainly says that different living creatures will come forth according to their own kind and not from one common ancestor of all. He then defines what He means by enumerating the creatures: "cattle and creeping thing and beast of the earth," rendering impossible the paradigm that everything came from a different creature smaller and simpler than itself. The *Theological Wordbook of the Old Testament* explains:

> Some have argued that when God created "min" [class, kind, species], he thereby fixed the "species." This is a gratuitous assumption because a link between the word "min" with the biologist's descriptive term "species" cannot be substantiated, and because there are as many definitions of species as there are biologists ... God created the basic forms of life called "min" which can be classified according to modern biologists and zoologists as sometimes species, sometimes genus, sometimes family or sometimes order. This gives no support to the classical evolutionist's view which requires developments across kingdom, phyla, and classes.

Dogs Are Still Dogs

Animals reproducing fertile offspring according to their own kind is what we see in nature. We see hundreds of varieties of dogs, but dogs are still dogs. This (largely human-caused) variation in dogs is often called evolution. This is reflected in the *Seed Magazine* article "The Human-Influenced Evolution of Dogs" (Anthes 2006), which discusses not the molecules-to-man type of evolution of how a non-dog turned into a dog, but how through human intervention "the domestication of dogs by humans has given rise to the immense diversity of the canine species by allowing otherwise harmful genetic mutations to survive" (Anthes 2006). This "evolution" that Anthes refers to is nothing more than variation within a kind. Nevertheless, she is echoed by the Natural History Museum in London which says that the breeding of dogs shows evolution as well (Batten 1996). Here again, we are given an example of Natural Selection (adaptation and variation, which are factual and observed) and are led to believe that it is equivalent to molecules-to-man evolution.

However, there is no "evolution" of the dog at all, other than variation due greatly to humans. Interestingly, the study of genetics confirms that all dogs have come from a common ancestry. "Most breeds have developed during the past 500 years, [...] Before humans began breeding dogs for certain traits or behaviors, dogs were more general in their appearance or morphology [...]" (Dalke 2002). The multiplicity of dogs is not a proof of evolution but of dog's best friend manipulating him to better suit man. "Breeds tell us more about human preferences than about dogs [...] Dog breeds are the result of human preferences—selected traits taken from generation to generation" (Dalke 2002). "The Human-Influenced Evolution of Dogs" would be better titled "Man's Breeding of Dogs."

Views of Biblical Creation

For those holding to the belief that God was the agent of creation, there are four possible answers to the question of how He did it. The first view is that God took six literal days as understood by the plain reading of the Genesis text, which is the thesis of this book. The other three views consider the evolutionary model to be an established fact and therefore seek to reconcile the revelation of Scripture regarding creation with evolution. The three views are Theistic Evolution, the Gap Theory, and Progressive Creationism.

Theistic Evolution

Theistic Evolution is the most liberal of the views that ascribes to God a role in creation as being the agent that jump-started the Big Bang. According to this theory, since then He has allowed evolution to take its course thereby having very little, if any, role in His creation and dealings with man.

The Gap Theory

Proponents of the Gap Theory see the days of Genesis 1 as being literal days but with a time gap between Genesis 1:1 and 1:2 (some also suggest a gap between 1:2 and 1:3). The rationale for seeking a gap, nevertheless, is due to the belief that (geological) evolution is an established fact and that the Bible must be reconciled to it. Hence, a time gap is envisioned between Genesis 1:1 and 1:2 (or 1:2–1:3), which allows for the billions of years supposedly necessary for geological evolution to take place.

Progressive Creationism

Progressive Creationism seeks to reconcile the belief of evolution with the Bible, not by way of a gap between verses 1:1 and 1:2, but rather by redefining six days of Genesis 1 to mean indefinite periods of time in which millions and perhaps billions of years transpired each *day*. They see God as being involved in the entire process of creation wherein every day, God was creating via the evolutionary process.[8] Van Bebber and Taylor point out:

> According to the Progressive Creationist timeline, Adam was, in effect, created on top of a graveyard of decaying or fossilized animals. Almost anywhere he walked, the remains of millions of dead animals were somewhere below his feet—evidence of death and frequent misery on a massive scale (2006).

Thus, for the Progressive Creationist, both the Bible and the evolutionary model complement one another because the biblical creation account is better understood through the lens of evolutionary thinking. Undoubtedly, most proponents of both the Gap Theory and Progressive Creationism believe in the authority of the Bible.

How Much Time Does God Need?

Rather than ask why couldn't God have taken billions of years to accomplish His work of creation, the better question is why didn't God speak once and everything merely come into existence as suggested by Augustine (see chapter 7)? God, the Supreme Being by whom all things exist, could have snapped His divine fingers and everything would have come into being at once. Thus, even from a literal, six-day-creation standpoint, God took His time in a big way! Why did He take so long to create everything? God purposely slowed Himself down rather than just getting it over with. The reason, found in Exodus 20:11 (and 31:12–17), is that God wanted to establish a pattern which for mankind to follow; God worked for six days and then rested and so should man.

3-The "Fact" of Evolution

A large number of well-trained scientists outside of evolutionary biology and paleontology have unfortunately gotten the idea that the fossil record is far more Darwinian than it is. This probably comes from the oversimplification inevitable in secondary sources: low-level textbooks, semi-popular articles, and so on. Also, there is probably some wishful thinking involved. In the years after Darwin, his advocates hoped to find predictable progressions. In general, these have not been found—yet the optimism has died hard, and some pure fantasy has crept into textbooks [...] (David Raup 1981: 832, professor of Geology, University of Chicago, Chicago Field Museum, emphasis mine).

The primary reason that there is any question regarding the length of the creation days of Genesis is due to many people's belief that evolution is a fact, and since it is a *fact*, then a literal reading of Genesis must not be valid. Some have gone so far as to suggest that the ancient Israelites were simplistic and merely ignorant of true science, which is precisely what medical doctor William Keen did in his 1922 book entitled *I Believe in God and Evolution*. Keen's book may be somewhat dated, but the attitude he championed has not changed. In fact, we could argue it has become even more entrenched today.

Fully convinced that evolution was an established fact, Keen argued, "A fundamental difficulty with the so called 'Fundamentalists' is that they fail to recognize the fact that the 'children of Israel' … were living in the intellectual childhood of the human race" (Keen 1922: 7). He then goes on with his biased and incorrect version of ancient history by stating, "… their minds were cast in a poetic mold, their literature was permeated with imagery, metaphors and parables. Bards, priests and prophets delivered it to them. No scientists then existed" (Keen 1922: 8).

Neither of Keen's observations is based on historical fact. Unfortunately, his belief in evolution has skewed his understanding of history, though his perspective is consistent with the evolutionary model. Simply stated, the evolutionary model proposes that life-forms continue to get more and more complex and so too does man's sophistication and understanding of the world. While mankind is more technologically advanced today than ever before, and hence we have more and usually better data to work with, ancient man was by no means primitive, nor was man at that time in the "intellectual childhood of the human race."

The age before Abraham (approximately 2000 BC) saw amazing applications of scientific principles based on math, geometry, physics, etc. The ancient civilizations of the time (the Sumerians, Babylonians, Akkadians, and Egyptians) were the ones who invented writing, an extremely complex concept not for the weak-minded. These civilizations first developed elaborate mathematical tables. It was even the Babylonians[9] who preempted the Greek philosopher Pythagoras with his famous discovery known as the Pythagorean Theorem by approximately 1,300 years (O'Connor and Robertson 2000b). These ancient peoples erected enormous pyramids and ziggurats, which to this day still defy some of our best engineering prowess— and they did so all without the aid of motorized machinery. They plotted the course of the stars with incredible precision and devised extremely accurate calendars. They wrote music and plays for entertainment, kept immaculate business records that have survived until today, and even had a postal system. This supposedly primitive culture, to which Keen referred, codified extensive laws, which in many countries, law students are still required to study.

Keen is equally incorrect in claiming that there were no scientists. Let's consider some evidence that shows that ancient man was actually quite advanced and therefore was not mentally primitive as Keen as suggested. If men were not mentally primitive, then they were able to faithfully and accurately pass down the creation account given to them by God.

What Is Science?

The *Collins English Dictionary* defines *science* as "the systematic study of the nature and behavior of the material and physical universe, based on observation, experiment, and measurement, and the formulation of laws to describe these facts in general terms." This description certainly applies to what we narrowly define as science today. But the word *science* comes from Latin and simply means *knowledge*. This meaning is reflected in the *Webster's Dictionary* 1828 definition, "In a general sense, knowledge, or certain knowledge; the comprehension or understanding of truth or facts by the mind." The Bible contains many astute observations about nature that demonstrate that the authors were very observant of the world around them and came to conclusions about their world.

In the book of Job, we find a statement that claims something that was not universally accepted in the ancient world. Whereas the countries surrounding Israel believed that the world was either floating on water or founded upon the body of a dead or living god, the Bible describes the earth suspended in empty space: "He stretches out the north over empty space; He hangs the earth on nothing על־בלי־מה [*al-bli-ma* literally: *on-without-what*]" (Job 26:7).

Ecclesiastes 1 verses 6 and 7, thought to have been written by Solomon, make keen observations regarding the circulation of the atmosphere and the water cycle:

> The wind goes toward the south,
> And turns around to the north;
> The wind whirls about continually,
> And comes again on its circuit.
> All the rivers run into the sea,
> Yet the sea is not full;
> To the place from which the rivers come,
> There they return again.

We take these passages for granted since they communicate things that are fairly common knowledge today, but these passages demonstrate an extraordinary understanding of the world—all without the benefit of high-tech measuring instruments. At the most, these are proofs that God inspired the words of the Bible; and at the least, they demonstrate good science on man's behalf. Consider another example:

> The birds of the air,
> And the fish of the sea
> That pass through the paths of the seas (Psalm 8:8).

The fact that "the seas were circulating systems with interaction between wind and water"[10] was not known until the late 1800s, yet the Bible contained this truth almost three thousand years earlier than modern science. In essence, William Keen and those in agreement today who claim that the Bible is just a collection of myths and therefore we need not take it literally but instead must interpret the Bible by way of modern science, have made a grave mistake. The Bible is reliable and scientific. Certainly, if indeed inspired by God, then it must be accurate. However, if only inspired by men, then those men were first-rate scientists of their day. Dr. Keen's thesis is certainly not unique, however. In fact, it seems that the number of individuals who claim, "I Believe in God and Evolution" only grows in spite of the authority and accuracy of the Bible.

Evolution Sunday

On February 12, 2006, hundreds of churches around the United States observed Evolution Sunday, a celebration of the 197th birthday of Charles Darwin, in order to support the teaching of evolution in public schools. Evolution Sunday was the culmination of approximately two years of gathering signatures from over ten thousand clergy from many mainline churches who believe that evolution is an established fact. "At St. Dunstan's Episcopal Church, Atlanta, the Rev. Patricia Templeton told the 85 worshipers [...] 'A faith that requires you to close your mind in order to believe is not much of a faith at all'" (*New York Times*, February 13, 2006). A parishioner from that church commented in a similar fashion:

> Observation, hypothesis and testing—that's what science is, it's not religion. Evolution is a fact. It's not a theory. An example is antibiotics. If we don't use antibiotics appropriately, bacteria become resistant. That's evolution, and evolution is a fact (ibid).

Unfortunately Rev. Patricia Templeton and her parishioners have misunderstood both the Bible and science. She is wrong in believing that the teaching of the Bible somehow requires us to close our minds—the Bible actually gives us the correct paradigm with which to properly understand the world. It tells us why people behave selfishly and sinfully, why there is disease and death, and why we see the scars of a global cataclysm known as the flood. The real scientific evidence, as we will see, supports the Bible.

The parishioner that made the above statement is wrong as well since he lacks a basic understanding of the difference between macro and Natural Selection. Natural Selection, speciation, and adaptation are embraced by essentially all Bible believers. The person referred to merely an example of how organisms adapt to their surroundings—a fact which is recognized by all. As noted, Darwin was correct in observing the change of the beaks of the finches. That, however, was all that he actually observed. The other aspects of his model are speculation and not based on "observation, hypothesis and testing," the very requirements people claim the Bible leaves out.

Molecules-to-man evolution, that is to say the changing of one kind to another (reptile to bird, for instance), remains nothing more than a paradigm which has never been observed and cannot by any means be proven even after so many years of trying. It is not an established fact. Darwin himself even wrote in a letter[11] to Asa Gray, a Harvard professor of biology, "I am quite conscious that my speculations run quite beyond the bounds of true science." Darwin was not the only "Darwinist" to recognize this point. L. H. Matthews wrote in the Introduction to Darwin's (1971 edition) *Origin of the Species*:

> The fact of evolution is the backbone of biology and biology is thus in the peculiar position of being **a science founded on unproven theory**. Is it then a science or a faith? **Belief in the theory of evolution is thus exactly parallel to belief in special creation.** Both are concepts which the believers know to be true, but neither, up to the present, has been capable of proof[12] (emphasis mine).

Matthews is by far not the only person to suggest such sentiments regarding the scarcity of evidence in support of the evolutionary model. Famed evolutionist Stephen J. Gould of Harvard stated, "The evolutionary trees that adorn our textbooks have data only at the tips and nodes of their branches; the rest is inference, however reasonable, not the evidence of the fossils" (1990: 13). David M. Raup, paleontologist at the University of Chicago and curator and Dean of Science at the Chicago Field Museum of Natural History, likewise stated:

> The evidence we find in the geologic record is not nearly as compatible with Darwinian natural selection as we would like it to be. Darwin was completely aware of this. He was embarrassed by the fossil record

because it didn't look the way he predicted it would [...]. Well, we are now about 120 years after Darwin and the knowledge of the fossil record has been greatly expanded. We now have a quarter of a million fossil species but the situation hasn't changed much. [...] **Ironically, we have even fewer examples of evolutionary transition than we had in Darwin's time.** By this I mean that some of **the classic cases of Darwinian change** in the fossil record, such as the evolution of the horse in North America, **have had to be discarded or modified** as the result of more detailed information (Raup 1979: 22–29, emphasis mine).

The Clergy Letter Project

The Clergy Letter Project from which the idea of Evolution Sunday came about issued the following statement (An Open Letter Concerning Religion and Science) that sadly claims that the keystone and foundational passages of Genesis are nothing more than stories with a spiritual message and are not real historical events. The entire letter has been copied below:

> Within the community of Christian believers there are areas of dispute and disagreement, including the proper way to interpret Holy Scripture. While virtually all Christians take the Bible seriously and hold it to be authoritative in matters of faith and practice, the overwhelming majority do not read the Bible literally, as they would a science textbook. Many of the beloved stories found in the Bible—the Creation, Adam and Eve, Noah and the ark—convey timeless truths about God, human beings, and the proper relationship between Creator and creation expressed in the only form capable of transmitting these truths from generation to generation. **Religious truth is of a different order from scientific truth. Its purpose is not to convey scientific information but to transform hearts.**

We the undersigned, Christian clergy from many different traditions, believe that the timeless truths of the Bible and the discoveries of modern science may comfortably coexist. **We believe that the theory of evolution is a foundational scientific truth,** one that has stood up to rigorous scrutiny and upon which much of human knowledge and achievement rests. To reject this truth or to treat it as "one theory among others" is to deliberately embrace scientific ignorance and transmit such ignorance to our children. We believe that among God's good gifts are human minds capable of critical thought and that the failure to fully employ this gift is a rejection of the will of our Creator. To argue that God's loving plan of salvation for humanity precludes the full employment of the God-given faculty of reason is to attempt to limit God, an act of hubris. We urge school board members to preserve the integrity of the science curriculum by affirming the teaching of the theory of evolution as a core component of human knowledge. **We ask that science remain science and that religion remain religion, two very different, but complementary, forms of truth** ("An Open Letter Concerning Religion and Science," Clergy Letter Project, 2004, emphasis mine).

What Kind of Truths Are the Biblical Promises?

Whether or not religious truth is different than scientific truth is irrelevant; if something is indeed true, then it does not matter what category it falls into. The events as described in the Bible are either true or they are not; there can be no middle ground.

The very accounts that they are dismissing as being spiritual stories or allegories are, in fact, the very foundation of the Bible. For example, if the flood did not actually occur as Genesis declares, then the promise given by God "I have sworn that the waters of Noah would no longer cover the earth ..." (Isaiah 54:9) through the prophet Isaiah is worthless. If God based His promise on an event that did not really occur, then what assurance would outcast Israel have that someday God would no longer hide His face but restore them?

> "For a mere moment I have forsaken you, but with great mercies I will gather you. With a little wrath I hid My face from you for a moment; but with everlasting kindness I will have mercy on you," says the LORD, your Redeemer. "For this is like the waters of Noah to Me; **for as I have sworn that the waters of Noah would no longer cover the earth,** so have I sworn that I would not be angry with you, nor rebuke you. For the mountains shall depart and the hills be removed, but My kindness shall not depart from you, nor shall My covenant of peace be removed," says the LORD, who has mercy on you (Isaiah 54:7–10, emphasis mine).

God is comparing the judgment of the earth by the flood with the judgment on Israel. Here He promises that just as the waters would no longer cover the earth, which is to say that the judgment would not happen again, so too was the promise that Israel's judgment would pass. If the story of the flood is just a timeless story to teach us about God, what do we do with the promise that He made to Israel? If there was no real flood, was there also not a real judgment that fell on them? Clearly from biblical and secular history we know that is not true; Israel definitely was judged as we will see in the statements of Daniel, Jeremiah, and the Chronicler. Later in chapter 11 we will look at some real-world evidence of that flood.

Furthermore, if we categorize the creation account, Adam and Eve, and Noah and the Flood as being merely figurative and non-literal stories that contain truths, all the while denying that they are in fact true in what they state about cosmology, history, and geology, then what do we do with the promise of redemption given to us concerning the current sinful condition of man?

Is Jesus the fulfillment of that promise? Was there really ever a promise made? And if there was a promise made, then to whom was it made if not to the real, historical Adam and real, historical Eve? Gleason Archer stated well the importance of the Bible being true and accurate in all areas that it touches: "If the biblical record can be proved fallible in areas of fact that can be verified, then it is hardly to be trusted in areas where it cannot be tested" (Archer 1982: 23).

Darwin Didn't Want God's Help

We should not use man's observation of nature to interpret the Bible. Man sees things differently every day and in a way that fits his best interests. The data concerning the origin of the universe are out there, but how we interpret those data is the true test. After having seen the historical and archeological confirmations of Scripture, we should therefore let Scripture be the starting point of our worldview. We ought not let man's interpretation of nature be used to interpret Scripture.

Accepting the various facets of the evolutionary model as fact is the only reason for arguing that the creation days mean billions of years. Ironically, Darwinian evolution is diametrically opposed to God's assisting in any way. It is given as a plausible mechanism for how we are here *without* any first cause, not how God might have done the job! There seems to have been no room for divine intervention in Darwin's world. Darwin expert Neal Gillespie noted "Darwin clearly rejected Christianity and virtually all conventional arguments in defense of the existence of God and human immortality" (Gillespie 1974: 141).

Furthermore, Sir Arthur Keith stated in the introduction to the sixth edition (1872) of Charles Darwin's *Origin of the Species by Means of Natural Selection*:

> [...] we see that Darwin's aim was to replace a belief
> in special creation by a belief in evolution and in this
> he did succeed, as every modern biologist will readily
> admit (Keith 1872: xvi–xvii).

Darwin himself, in *Life and Letters of Charles Darwin* published posthumously, describes the process by which he went from a belief in God to removing God from his world completely:

> Thus disbelief crept over me at a very slow rate, but was at last complete. The rate was so slow that I felt no distress, and have never since doubted even for a single second that my conclusion was correct. I can indeed hardly see how anyone ought to wish Christianity to be true (Darwin 1896: 274–286).

Evidently, to grant room for evolution in Genesis is contrary to what Darwin advocated. If Darwin didn't believe in Theistic Evolution, why should we? Before looking at the actual text of Genesis we first need to consider what method should be used to interpret those days of creation.

4-Interpreting Genesis

> As for me, when I hear the word "grass" I think of grass, and the same with plant, fish, wild beast, domestic animal. I take everything in the literal sense, for "I am not ashamed of the Gospel" (Basil, Church Father, fourth century).

The Method of Interpreting the Bible

Correctly understanding the six days of creation ultimately comes down to how we approach the Scriptures. A frequent accusation against the Bible is that one can make it say whatever one wants. Unquestionably there are people who take such liberty and try to make the Bible fit into their philosophies. However, is it true that the Bible allows for such liberties? Is God's Word really so ambiguous? Or is there a method to properly understand and capture the message that He intended for us to receive? The importance of this question is staggering because where one begins will often determine where one ends up. If our method of interpretation is so fluid that the Bible can say anything, then it generally will. However, if our method assumes that what is said is what is meant, then we will arrive at trustworthy conclusions not based on how clever we are in our interpretation, but on our simply reading and believing what the text says.

This type of interpretation is known as the grammatical-historical method. It assumes that the words and thoughts that are conveyed in the Bible are used in the same way that normal speech, writing, and conversation occur in everyday life. Basically stated, we don't have to read between the lines of the Bible to understand what it means. The greatest advantage of interpreting the Bible in a straightforward manner is that we are able to test our conclusions regarding what it says against archeology, historical documents, and examination of the Hebrew and Greek grammar of the particular passage.

Scripture Interprets Scripture

The wonder of the Bible is that we use Scripture to interpret Scripture based on the words of Jesus in John 10:35, where he said "… and Scripture cannot be broken." The apostles Paul and Peter reiterate this:

> All Scripture is given by inspiration of God, and is profitable for doctrine, for reproof, for correction, for instruction in righteousness (1 Timothy 3:16).

> […] as also our beloved brother Paul, according to the wisdom given to him, has written to you, as also in all his epistles, speaking in them of these things, in which are some things hard to understand, which untaught and unstable people twist to their own destruction, as they do **also the rest of the Scriptures** (2 Peter 3:15–16, emphasis mine).

Notice that Peter equates the writings of Paul with "the rest of the Scriptures," that is, the Old Testament. Since Peter considers the writings of Paul to be inspired by God as those of the Old Testament, which were obviously considered authoritative, we can confidently use the entire Bible to help interpret the meaning of *days* in Genesis 1.

Using the Bible to interpret itself is not circular reasoning. The Bible is not just one single document written by one author at one time. Rather, it is a collection of sixty-six books written by forty authors over a period of about 1,500 years. As a teacher of the Bible trained at the secular, humanistic Hebrew University of Jerusalem, I am well aware of its critics. Therefore, I take great interest in making sure that our approach to interpreting Scripture be consistent. The fact that the Bible is a compilation of many books by many authors over the period of 1,500 years and that its message is unified permits us to cross-reference its various books. Thus, when we use one portion of Scripture to interpret another, we are not just performing a tautological exercise. Rather we are referencing ancient documents and comparing those to other ancient documents.

Hermeneutics

This discipline of interpretation is formally called hermeneutics, which is how we decide what the Bible, or any text for that matter, actually means. Many people take a very relaxed view of interpreting the Bible; they subscribe to a type of moral relativism. However, they would fight tooth and nail when it comes to something like their portion of an inheritance as defined in a will, or how much money is owed according to a legal contract.

In the above cases, no one would be looking for a hidden meaning but would look at the plain meaning of the text. No competent judge would try to "read between the lines" in order to make a will, contract, insurance claim, or our bank balance say something that it really doesn't say—and if a judge did such a thing, we would all cry "injustice!!"

What Do We Mean By Literal?

Just as the normal method of understanding everyday letters, contracts, and documents is literal, straightforward, and uses the historical-grammatical approach rather than the allegorical approach, this is also the method we use to interpret the Bible. This does not mean that the biblical authors did not occasionally use metaphors, similes, analogies, and once in a while even allegory to teach a point.

John, in the book of Revelation, sees a vision in heaven where Jesus is referred to as a lamb and also as a lion (Revelation 5:5–6). Other times Jesus Himself states that He is the Bread of heaven (John 6:51), the Door (John 10:7), the Good Shepherd (John 10:11), etc. Does this mean that we cannot understand the text or that everything is to be taken allegorically? By no means! Jesus is making illustrations about Himself in order to teach an important lesson. They are all true in the context of what He was teaching. We would never assume that Jesus is actually flour, salt, and water, the ingredients in literal bread, nor would we think that He is a piece of wood as a door, nor even a four-footed creature as John saw in Revelation. We understand that He is speaking figuratively. However, there are real truths behind what He was saying. Jesus frequently used parables, a type of allegory to teach certain truths, yet there was no question that it was a story. There was no thought that Jesus was actually communicating a real, historical event. Telling stories (parables) was a very Jewish way of teaching employed by many rabbis of Jesus' day.

What Is Allegory?

We have spoken of the grammatical-historical method of interpretation and have suggested that it is the normal method to be employed. What is the allegorical method and why should we avoid interpreting the Bible in such a manner? J. Dwight Pentecost addresses this manner of interpreting Scripture in great detail in his classic work *Things to Come*. "In this method the historical import is either denied or ignored and the emphasis is placed entirely on a secondary sense so that the original words or events have little or no significance" (Pentecost 1958: 4). He also cites Ramm who defines allegory as "… the method of interpreting a literary text that regards the literal sense as the vehicle for a secondary, more spiritual and more profound sense" (Ramm 1950: 1). Pentecost summarizes this by saying that "it would seem that the purpose of the allegorical method is not to interpret Scripture, but to pervert the true meaning of

Scripture, albeit under the guise of seeking a deeper or more spiritual meaning" (Pentecost 1958: 5).

Dr. Pentecost points out three dangers of the allegorical method:

1. The first great danger of the allegorical method is that it does not interpret Scripture.

2. The basic authority in interpretation ceases to be the Scriptures, but the mind of the interpreter. The interpretation may then be twisted by the interpreter's doctrinal positions, the authority of the church to which the interpreter adheres, his social or educational background, or a host of other factors.

3. [...] one is left without any means by which the conclusions of the interpreter may be tested (Pentecost 1958: 5–6).

An example of allegory is found in Galatians 4:24–26 where Paul plainly tells us that he is using an allegory and he then gives us the meaning behind those symbols. We are not left to dig for a deeper hidden meaning, nor are we to address every Old Testament passage looking for the "real" truth behind the text. Paul is taking real, historical events significant in their own right and is simply drawing out a typology to teach a spiritual truth.

> [...] which things are symbolic [ἀλληγορούμενα—*allegory*]. For these are the two covenants: the one from Mount Sinai which gives birth to bondage, which is Hagar—for this Hagar is Mount Sinai in Arabia, and corresponds to Jerusalem which now is, and is in bondage with her children—but the Jerusalem above is free, which is the mother of us all.

The above example is not truly the employment of the allegorical method, but rather the explanation of an allegory (Pentecost 1958: 7). We can be sure that Paul is not using the allegorical method of interpretation because he did not deny the historicity of the Old Testament account, but merely employed the story as an illustration.

The real issue between a literal and an allegorical method of interpretation is in essentially knowing how God communicated with His people in Scripture. Did He communicate in such a way that one had to read between the lines to truly get at what He was saying? Or did He generally use plain language that was easy for mankind to understand? What was God's normal method of communication?

There are numerous examples of where the Bible interprets itself in very clear language leaving no doubt whatsoever as to its intent. An example is found in Genesis where God declares that man may eat from any tree except from the Tree of the Knowledge of Good and Evil. Regardless of which method of interpretation we use, we see that behind God's words was a very real consequence. According to Genesis and the rest of the Bible, man's decision to eat of the tree had very real consequences not to be undone until the end of time when the tree of life is restored (Revelation 22:2). At least from the Bible's standpoint, God's words were to be taken literally; to understand otherwise would confuse the entire message of the Bible. Let's consider in detail the accounts of Moses and Daniel to see which method of interpretation they employed.

Striking the Rock

The children of Israel's wandering in the wilderness offers an example of where several biblical writers interpret in a literal fashion. After fleeing from Egypt through the wilderness, they came to a place where they had no water. God commanded Moses to strike the rock so that water would come out of it (Exodus 17:6). Moses did so, and as a result, water gushed forth from the rock providing life-giving water to the thirsty Israelites. This episode is recounted hundreds of years later as a historical fact by the Psalmist Asaph in Psalm 78 where he declares:

Give ear, O my people, to my law; Incline your ears to the words of my mouth. [...] we have heard and known [...] our fathers have told us. For He [...] appointed a law in Israel, which He commanded our fathers, that they should make them known to their children [...] And His wonders that He had shown them. Marvelous things He did in the sight of their fathers, in the land of Egypt [...] He divided the sea and caused them to pass through; and He made the waters stand up like a heap. In the daytime also He led them with the cloud, and all the night with a light of fire. **He split the rocks in the wilderness,** and gave them drink in abundance like the depths. **He also brought streams out of the rock,** and caused waters to run down like rivers (Psalm 78:1, 3, 5, 7, and 11–16, emphasis mine).

Asaph uses concrete words to describe the historical fact of the rock being struck and water coming out, such as: "we have heard," "our fathers have told us," "(God) appointed a law ... to make known." He makes it abundantly clear, that he, at least, believed that the striking of the rock was a very real, historical event and that the events occurred as stated. There is no sense of allegory whatsoever in his language. The striking of the rock and water coming forth is reiterated in Psalm 105:41 where another psalmist states: "He opened the rock, and water gushed out; It ran in the dry places like a river." Both of these writers have interpreted the events in Exodus literally and straightforwardly.

Years later, in the Exodus story, they encountered another place where there was no water. God then told Moses to *speak* to the rock, rather than *hit* it. Moses, extremely frustrated with these people who seemed to never stop complaining, struck the rock, rather than speaking to it as God commanded. As a result of Moses' moment of wrath, he was not allowed to enter into the Promised Land. God's reasoning for doing so was that Moses had not represented God accurately to the people. God was not angry with the people, although Moses had communicated just the opposite through his actions. God's words were given plainly, "Speak to the rock" (Numbers 20:8). Moses disobeyed and so there was a real consequence. "Then the LORD spoke to Moses and Aaron, 'Because you did not believe Me, to hallow Me in the eyes of the children of Israel, therefore you shall not bring this assembly into the land which I have given them'" (Numbers 20:12).

We later find in the New Testament that Paul uses this real, historical event to teach a spiritual truth. He claims the Rock to be Christ—that is Christ is He who satisfies our true spiritual thirst. In fact, according to ancient Jewish sources, the rock was believed to have physically traveled with the children of Israel.[13] Nevertheless he never questions the original account's historicity:

> Moreover, brethren, I do not want you to be unaware that all **our fathers were under the cloud, all passed through the sea**, all were baptized into Moses in the cloud and in the sea, all ate the same spiritual food, and all drank the same spiritual drink. For they drank of that spiritual Rock that followed them, and that Rock was Christ. But with most of them God was not well pleased, **for their bodies were scattered in the wilderness**. Now these things became our examples, to the intent that we should not lust after evil things as they also lusted (1 Corinthians 10:1–6, emphasis mine).

Paul obviously thought that these events actually did occur and were not just metaphors or allegories because he says that the fathers truly were under the cloud and did pass through the sea, but God was not happy with them and, consequently, their dead bodies were all over the desert. He says that they became examples so that we should not do as they did. Thus Paul discusses Jesus as the Rock to teach a truth, but he in no way questions the historicity of the actual events. He rather confirms that those things indeed happened and exhorts the Corinthians not to follow suit.

Daniel

Jeremiah's 70 Years

In 606 BC, the Neo-Babylonian king, Nebuchadnezzar the Second, came to Jerusalem and took away a portion of its inhabitants captive to Babylon for failure to pay the necessary tribute. This first deportation in 606 BC was followed by another in 597 BC and then a third, which culminated in the destruction of Jerusalem in 586 BC. During this time, the prophet Jeremiah was acting as the voice of the Lord toward a rebellious people. In spite of the tremendous castigation falling on His people, God gave Jeremiah a word of encouragement.

> And this whole land shall be a desolation and an astonishment, and these nations shall serve the king of Babylon **seventy years**. "Then it will come to pass, when **seventy years** are completed, that I will punish the king of Babylon and that nation, the land of the Chaldeans, for their iniquity," says the LORD; "and I will make it a perpetual desolation. So I will bring on that land all My words which I have pronounced against it, all that is written in this book, which Jeremiah has prophesied concerning all the nations" (Jeremiah 25:11–13, emphasis mine).

God Himself says that He would set them free after seventy years. There are two important things to notice here. There is absolutely no question that the Judeans went into captivity—that is established historical fact. There is also no question that in 539 BC Cyrus the Great conquered Babylon and then three years later, in 536 BC the Jews were allowed to return to Jerusalem to begin rebuilding the Temple—both are historical facts.

Daniel's Understanding of the 70 Years

In Daniel chapter 9, we see that Daniel, a biblical writer, interprets Jeremiah's prophecy for us. He sets the stage by telling when in history this chapter occurs: "In the first year of Darius the son of Ahasuerus, of the lineage of the Medes, who was made king over the realm of the Chaldeans" (Daniel 9:1). It is established historical fact that Darius the Mede existed and was governor over Babylon. Daniel then tells us that he was reading the prophet Jeremiah, who had written approximately seventy years earlier: "In the first year of his reign I, Daniel, understood by the books the number of the years specified by the word of the LORD through Jeremiah the prophet, that He would accomplish **seventy** years in the desolations of Jerusalem" (Daniel 9:2, emphasis mine). Here we have Daniel interpreting the prophecy of Jeremiah in unmistakable terms—he understood from the prophet Jeremiah that God would keep His people in Babylon for **seventy** literal years. Daniel does not try to look for a hidden message as to what God meant by seventy years or punishing Babylon, he assumes it to be literal. And judging from history, we can conclude that was indeed the case. Exactly seventy years after the first deportation, the Jews were allowed to return to Jerusalem.

Moved by the nearness of the fulfillment of prophecy, Daniel sets his face "toward the Lord God to make request by prayer and supplications, with fasting, sackcloth, and ashes. And I prayed to the LORD my God, and made confession ..." (Daniel 9:3). Daniel confesses the sins of his people to the Lord, acknowledging that they have not sought God's face and have received exactly what they deserved although God would be gracious enough to restore them after seventy years. He then confirms that the curse given in Deuteronomy was 100 percent literally fulfilled through the destruction of Jerusalem.

> "But it shall come to pass, if you do not obey the voice of the LORD your God, to observe carefully all His commandments and His statutes which I command you today, that all these curses will come upon you and overtake you [...] The LORD will send on you cursing, confusion, and rebuke in all that you set your hand to do, until you are destroyed and until you perish quickly,

because of the wickedness of your doings in which you have forsaken Me" (Deuteronomy 28:15, 20).

It was not just true in a spiritual sense, but came to pass in a very real and literal sense, at least as far as Daniel was concerned. He in no way intimated that the curses were mere spiritual consequences of not following God, but that they were specific to the nation of Israel exclusively and that they had been completely fulfilled.

> "Yes, all Israel has transgressed Your law, and has departed so as not to obey Your voice; therefore the curse and the oath written in the Law of Moses the servant of God have been poured out on us, because we have sinned against Him. As it is written in the Law of Moses, all this disaster has come upon us; yet we have not made our prayer before the LORD our God, that we might turn from our iniquities and understand Your truth" (Daniel 9:11, 13).

The Chronicler Agreed

Daniel's comments are extremely important for the question of our method of interpretation. Daniel was much closer to and was a part of the writing of the Old Testament—less than seventy years after Jeremiah, less than two hundred from the time of Isaiah. His own writings are also considered canonical, inspired, and authoritative. If he took such writings as literal and straightforward, how much more should we? The literal interpretation of Daniel regarding Jeremiah's prophecy is also shared by the writer of 2 Chronicles in extremely plain language:

> And those who escaped from the sword he [Nebuchadnezzar] carried away to Babylon, where they became servants to him and his sons until the rule of the kingdom of Persia, **to fulfill the word of the LORD by the mouth of Jeremiah**, until the land had enjoyed her Sabbaths. As long as she lay desolate she kept Sabbath, to fulfill **seventy** years. Now in the

> first year of Cyrus king of Persia, that the word of
> the LORD by the mouth of **Jeremiah** might **be ful-
> filled**, the LORD stirred up the spirit of Cyrus king
> of Persia, so that he made a proclamation throughout
> all his kingdom, and also put it in writing, saying,
> Thus says Cyrus king of Persia: All the kingdoms
> of the earth the LORD God of heaven has given me.
> And He has commanded me to build Him a house at
> Jerusalem which is in Judah. Who is among you of
> all His people? May the LORD his God be with him,
> and let him go up! (2 Chronicles 36:20–23, emphasis
> mine).

The author of Chronicles emphatically stresses the point that after seventy years God freed His people *just as Jeremiah predicted*. There obviously was no question in the mind of the writer that this prophecy was fulfilled completely and literally. What we have here is merely one of countless examples of where numbers in the Bible are not given just to draw out a spiritual truth, which one would do using the allegorical method but rather they are used literally.

Undoubtedly, many clever meanings could be assigned to the number seventy. For example, certain Bible commentators have suggested that seven is the perfect number and ten represents completeness. Therefore, we could say that seventy is the perfect number of completion. This interpretation sounds rather erudite and sophisticated. It might even "minister" to people's hearts. In fact, there is no way to argue that the number seventy doesn't mean that. Maybe it is the number of "perfect comple-tion." This interpretation, however, is nothing more than the product of my imagination. The problem with applying the allegorical method of interpretation to the Bible is that it leaves interpretation up to the imagination of the Bible commenta-tor rather than the interpretation being drawn out of the Bible through the textual, historical, and linguistic constraints.

Interpreting Literary Genre

The above examples certainly provide weighty evidence in favor of a literal method of interpreting the Bible. However, there are passages in Scripture which should not be taken literally. Consider Isaiah's beautiful line, "For you shall go out with joy, and be led out with peace; the mountains and the hills shall break forth into singing before you, and all the trees of the field shall clap their hands" (55:12). Isaiah is using a literary form known as personification because I doubt that he, or God, intended to mean that the literal mountains would start singing or that the trees would actually take their branches and start clapping. Nevertheless, although he is using poetic language, the truth that he is telling is going to be very real. And when it happens, even creation, in a sense, will rejoice just as Paul alluded to in Romans 8:22. Thus, we recognize the literary genre, but still understand the real and accurate message it is conveying.

When looking at the Genesis creation account, a question that we must consider is its literary style: is it a literal and accurate, straightforward, and even chronological summary of the actual events, or is it simply using figurative, allegorical, metaphorical language to teach us timeless truths? John Nevins notes succinctly that there seems to be no consensus regarding what literary genre it is and that those wishing to assign the creation account to a genre of literature that is not literal seem to have a hidden agenda. They simply wish to:

> [...] affirm minimalistically that God is Creator. And that affirmation is meant to be a theological, nonscientific statement which has no impact on how the world and universe came into being and developed subsequently (Nevins 1994).

Obviously, those who believe evolution to be God's mode of creation are forced to believe that Genesis is not a literal account, but full of metaphors, which they argue, are true in principle but not in the specific details in order for their belief about evolution to be true as well. Can we determine which category the Genesis account falls into?

What Is Meant by Literary Genre?

There are, broadly speaking, two literary genres (classes) in the Bible: prose and poetry. Prose simply means that the author is speaking in normal everyday language and is not attempting to speak poetically. Newspapers, history books, and even most emails employ prose, also known as narrative. Prose, however, contains many figures of speech, metaphors, similes, and the like. We can talk about the *sun going down* or *hungry as a horse*— both figures of speech that communicate a simple message; it is getting dark and I am hungry, respectively. In English there exist at least 440 animal sayings that we employ in our everyday language.[14] Expressions such as *you're barking up the wrong tree* or *it's raining cats and dogs* are certainly metaphors since my conversation partner is not truly outside barking at a tree in the park! Rather, I am using the metaphor to convey a real message: *you have got the wrong idea*. Likewise none of us has actually seen cats and dogs fall from the sky, it simply means that it is raining very hard. These expressions are considered prose and not poetry, which is defined as speaking or writing in such a manner where a particular rhyme, rhythm, cadence, or some other form of dramatic language is used to communicate.

Poetry in the Bible is occasionally marked making it easy to identify. Exodus 15:1 unmistakably states that a song (poetry) to the Lord is going to follow: "Then Moses and the children of Israel sang this **song** to the LORD, and spoke, saying …" Interestingly, Exodus 15 is the poetic form of chapter 14 which was written in prose—that is, a plain, straightforward kind of language. What we must not miss, however, is that both the prose account in chapter 14 and the poetic in 15 tell a true and historic account of what happened immediately prior in the departure from Egypt. Just because something is poetic does not mean that it is not also an accurate and historic account of what truly happened.

Scholars Believe in Literal Days of Genesis

Comparing different genre of literature in the Ancient Near East (the modern day Middle East) is a common method many Bible scholars use to determine a literary type. One such study on Genesis 1–11 noted, "we are dealing with the genre of historical narrative-prose, interspersed with some lists, sources, sayings, and poetical lines" (Kaiser 1970: 61). Kaiser includes Genesis 1 (and 2) in that description as well. That sentiment is echoed by eminent Old Testament scholar Gerhard von Rad, "The seven days are unquestionably to be understood as actual days […]" (von Rad 1972: 65). Many biblical scholars arguing on the basis of linguistic and literary criteria, while not trying to harmonize Genesis with evolution, see the days of Genesis 1 and 2 as literal, definite periods of time. Old Testament scholar Gordon Wenham states, "There can be little doubt that here 'day' has its basic sense of a 24-hour period" (Wenham 1987: 19). He is echoed by Oxford Hebrew Professor James Barr who does not actually believe Genesis but states emphatically regarding the writer's intent, "the creation 'days' were six literal days of a 144-hour period" (Barr 1978: 40). Barr later adds in a 1984 letter:

> […] probably, so far as I know, **there is no professor of Hebrew or Old Testament at any world-class university who does not believe** that the writer(s) of Genesis 1–11 intended to convey to their readers the ideas that:
>
> 1. Creation took place in a series of six days which were the same as the days of 24 hours we now experience.
>
> 2. The figures contained in the Genesis genealogies provided by simple addition a chronology from the beginning of the world up to later stages in the biblical story.
>
> 3. Noah's flood was understood to be world-wide and extinguish all human and animal life except for those in the ark (Barr 1984, emphasis mine).

John Nevins notes the impact of the testimony of liberal scholars:

> **Numerous scholars and commentators […] have concluded that the creation "days" cannot be anything but literal 24-hour days.** They are fully aware of the figurative, non-literal interpretations of the word "day" in Genesis 1 for the sake of harmonization with the long ages demanded by the evolutionary model of origins. Yet, **they insist on the grounds of careful investigations of the usage of "day" in Genesis 1 and elsewhere that the true meaning and intention of a creation "day" is a literal day of 24 hours** (Nevins 1994, emphasis mine).

Thus even scholars, many who hold to the evolutionary paradigm as the explanation for how the cosmos originated over that of the Bible, still believe that the creation account was written as a literal rendering of what the Genesis author believed to have happened. Many of the above scholars simply conclude that the Bible and science are at odds with no attempt made to synthesize the two. They do not believe that Genesis 1:1–2:3 is the actual explanation of where we came from but they do firmly believe that its author believed such and the days spoken of were thought to be literal and normal days just like the days of our time.

Final Thoughts Concerning Biblical Interpretation

In addition to the affirmation of a wide spectrum of biblical scholars that the biblical creation account was written to be understood literally, even in the pages of the Bible itself, we saw that its writers took God's words at face value. The author of Genesis took God's words about the eating of the fruit of the Tree of the Knowledge of Good and Evil as an event that had literal consequences. Moses was barred from entering into the Promised Land due to not obeying carefully, in every detail, God's instructions—evidence that God spoke literally and not figuratively. Furthermore, both Daniel and the writer of Chronicles demonstrated their literal understanding of several Scriptures. Essentially, we have seen from just a few examples that the normal method of biblical writers (when reading other Scripture passages) was to take them literally.

There are many other examples that could be examined such as the prophecies regarding the birth, death, and resurrection of Jesus. Every believer fully accepts those passages as being literally fulfilled in the person of Jesus. Even if one were to reject Jesus as Lord, one could not reject that the New Testament writers understood Jesus to be the literal fulfillment of hundreds of passages. The literal understanding of a coming messianic, divine, supernatural figure was shared by numerous Jews during the period of the Second Temple in addition to the disciples of Jesus and was later affirmed by all of the ante-Nicene Church Fathers. They were looking forward to a figure who would come and bring salvation from sins through His righteousness and then usher in a new era of peace under His divine rule on earth. If the prophecies regarding the first coming of Christ were and are taken literally, what is different when it comes to the days of Genesis? In fact Basil, a church father of the fourth century to whom we owe the correct understanding of the Trinity in contrast to the Arian heresy, boldly declares that the literal is the only right method of interpretation of Scripture.

> Those who do not accept the Scriptures in their ordinary, common meaning, say that "water" is not water but something else; plants and fishes they interpret as they please; the creation of reptiles and wild beasts they explain in their own way, twisting it from the obvious sense as do the interpreters of dreams—who give whatever meaning they choose to the images seen in sleep. As for me, when I hear the word "grass" I think of grass, and the same with plant, fish, wild beast, domestic animal. I take everything in the literal sense, for "I am not ashamed of the Gospel" (Basil, Hexaemeron, Homily IX).

5-The Question of "Days"

> For in six days the LORD made the heavens and the earth, the sea, and all that is in them, and rested the seventh day (Exodus 20:11).

The keystone of whether the earth is relatively young or extremely old rests heavily on the understanding of the Hebrew word יום *yom*, which is translated into English as *day*. The Progressive Creation theory which espouses the belief of an old earth (approximately 4.56 billion years old), while trying to remain faithful to Scripture, contends that the days in Genesis 1 (1:1–2:3) are to be understood as long, indefinite periods of time.

The young earth view, however, claims that God created the heavens and the earth and all therein in six literal 24-hour days *roughly* six thousand to ten thousand years ago. Who is to say who is right? How can we determine what a day really means? Does *day* only and always refer to a period of 24-hours or does it also refer to an indefinite period of time in which millions and billions of years could have passed allowing for the Progressive Creation and theistic-evolution theories?

Meanings of Day in the Old Testament

As with most misunderstandings in the Bible, the key to unlocking the puzzle lies in the context of the word. The word *day* is used in several different ways in the Bible. Occasionally, we see *days* referring to a time in the past. Judges 18:1, for example, states that "In those days ..." בימים ההם *bayamim hahem*. This exact phrase appears thirty-one times in the Old Testament. It is a very common expression and is really no different than how we in English say "back in my day" or "back in those days" referring to a period of years in our lives but stating it in *days*. Hence, in this context, days are understood to be referring to time in the past that probably lasted several years though definitely not thousands or millions—something that is obvious because it talks about human history of which the Bible gives definite times.

Sometimes the biblical writers used the word *day* to refer to a specific time that has theological or eschatological significance such as "the day of the LORD" *yom YHWH* יום הוה. This expression, found thirteen times in the Old Testament, mostly in the book of Isaiah, refers to a time in the future when God will judge the world and usher in a new age. This expression seems to speak more of an event of unknown duration rather than a specific amount of time, though a period of 24 hours cannot be ruled out.

At other times, *days* in the plural can refer to the span of someone's life. In Genesis 5:4 we read concerning the days of Adam, "So all the days that Adam (*yamei-adam* ימי־אדם) lived were nine hundred and thirty years; and he died." Here *day* is used in reference to Adam's lifetime, which is described as *days*, but then the text very clearly goes on to clarify what is meant by *days*—that is the years of his life or the summation of the days of his life. This is wonderfully illustrated by the Hebrew title of the book of 1 and 2 Chronicles דברי הימים למלכי ישראל *divre ha-yamim lemalche Israel*, literally transliterated as *affairs* or *matters of the days of the kings of Israel*.

24-Hour Days

The final meaning refers to days of 24-hours. The most basic way of defining a day was from evening to evening, which is indicated in the text by *evening and morning*. The ancient Israelites, contrary to us, started their new days at sunset. Thus, Friday night at sunset would already be considered the Sabbath and the day would end Saturday evening at around the same time.

Another way to indicate a regular day of 24-hours is by *hayom hazeh* היום הזה which is translated as "the very same day." In Genesis 7:13 we read: "On the very same day Noah [...] entered the ark." Likewise, Genesis 17:23 states: "So Abraham took Ishmael his son, all who were born in his house and all who were bought with his money, every male among the men of Abraham's house, and circumcised the flesh of their foreskins that very same day, as God had said to him." In both of these passages, the word *day* makes reference to the same day—that is the 24-hour period they were currently in. It is clear that the word here does not refer to an indefinite period of time but rather to a 24-hour period.

Days with a Cardinal Number

When a cardinal number (one, two, three, four, etc.) appears in front of the word *day*, it refers only and always to one (or many) period(s) of 24 hours. There are numerous verses which elucidate this point. Genesis 33:13 states:

> But Jacob said to him, "My lord knows that the children are weak, and the flocks and herds which are nursing are with me. And if the men should drive them hard one day, all the flock will die."

What Jacob is saying to his brother Esau is that there is a limit to how far little children and cattle can go in one day. The reference is clearly to one 24-hour period of time. Numbers 11:20 clarifies the usage even more. The children of Israel complained against the Lord because they did not have meat like they had in Egypt, the very place where God rescued them from. Rather than simply trust God for their needs or even ask for meat, they complained bitterly against God. In frustration with his stubborn children, He declares that they will have more meat than they know what to do with:

> "You shall eat, not one day, nor two days, nor five days, nor ten days, nor twenty days, but for a whole month, until it comes out of your nostrils and becomes loathsome to you, because you have despised the LORD Who is among you, and have wept before Him, saying, 'Why did we ever come up out of Egypt?'" (Numbers 11:20).

Here the meaning of *day* or *days* is clear. There will be not just one, or two, or five, or ten, or twenty days, but a whole month's worth of meat. The meaning of the word *day* is augmented by the contrast with the word "month" *chodesh* חודש, which only refers to the time of about thirty days or one cycle of the moon and never anything else.

Further proof that *yom day* refers to a 24-hour day when preceded by cardinal numbers is found throughout the Old Testament. God, in explaining the judgment coming upon the world, says in Genesis 7:4, "For after seven more days I will cause it to rain on the earth forty days and forty nights, and I will destroy from the face of the earth all living things that I have made." God gave Noah another seven days—not long, indefinite periods of time, but seven 24-hour days, until the floodwaters would come. Verse 10 records that indeed after seven literal days, the waters of the flood came: "And it came to pass after seven days that the waters of the flood were on the earth." Verse 11 surpasses the previous two in precision by telling us exactly when this occurred.

> In the six hundredth year of Noah's life, in the second month, the seventeenth day of the month, on that day all the fountains of the great deep were broken up, and the windows of heaven were opened.

This description is not just about some indefinite period of time. It was on the 17th of the second month, a very real time that the flood came. And then the record (verse 24) tells us specifically how long the waters were on the earth. "And the waters prevailed on the earth one hundred and fifty days." One hundred and fifty days in the text is not some long, undetermined era. Some people would contend that the days of the flood are irrelevant since Noah was simply a mythical or an allegorical figure. However, if one accepts the words of Jesus and the New Testament, then one must also accept that Noah was a real person who lived through the worldwide flood. (See Matthew 24:37–38, Luke 17:26–27, 1 Peter 3:20, 2 Peter 2:5, Hebrews 11:7.) Thus, because Jesus and the disciples accepted Noah as real, we must understand the days described in Genesis as being real, 24-hour days.

The list of verses in the Old Testament confirming that every time a number comes before day it is referring to a 24-hour day is extensive. A few more examples clearly illustrate the principle. "Then he put three days' journey between himself and Jacob, and Jacob fed the rest of Laban's flocks" (Genesis 30:36). "Forty days were required for him [Joseph], for such are the days required for those who are embalmed; and the Egyptians mourned for him seventy days" (Genesis 50:3). "And seven days passed after the LORD had struck the river" (Exodus 7:25). "Seven days you shall eat unleavened bread. On the first day you shall remove leaven from your houses. For whoever eats leavened bread from the first day until the seventh day, that person shall be cut off from Israel" (Exodus 12:15). "Six days you shall gather it, but on the seventh day, the Sabbath, there will be none" (Exodus 16:26). "So Gad came to David and told him; and he said to him, 'Shall seven years of famine come to you in your land? Or shall you flee three months before your enemies, while they pursue you? Or shall there be three days' plague in your land?'" (2 Samuel 24:13). Although there are too many verses to list here, throughout the entire Old Testament, in every case where a number precedes *day*, it deals with the literal usage of *day* rather than an indefinite period of time [see Appendix 2].

Days with Ordinal Numbers

A cardinal number before *day* is not the only way to express literal days. We see again and again that ordinal numbers (first, second, third, fourth, etc.) are also used in a literal sense when used with *day*. Ezekiel records that on a particular (literal) day of a particular month of a particular year God again spoke to him: "Again, in the ninth year, in the tenth month, on the **tenth day** of the month, the word of the LORD came to me" (Ezekiel 24:1, emphasis mine). Likewise, Ezra records the exact day when the temple was finished: "Now the temple was finished on the **third day** of the month of Adar, which was in the sixth year of the reign of King Darius" (Ezra 6:15, emphasis mine).

We find in the book of Numbers a usage of ordinal numbers that is parallel to Genesis 1. In Genesis 1 we saw the chronology of creation described as *one day* and then the *second day*, the *third day*, etc. In Numbers 29, God lists the various sacrifices and on which day they are to be performed for the Feast of Tabernacles. Notice that the days listed have the same ordinal numbers[15] as used in Genesis.

> On the **second day** (יום השני *yom hasheni*) present twelve young bulls, [...] On the **third day** (יום השלישי *yom hashlishi*) present eleven bulls, [...] On the **fourth day** (יום הרביעי *yom harevi'i*) present [...] On the **fifth day** (יום החמישי *yom hachamishi*) present [...] On the **sixth day** (יום השישי *yom hashishi*) present [...] On the **seventh day** (יום השביעי *yom hashvi'i*) present seven bulls (Numbers 29:17, 20, 23, 26, 29, 32, emphasis mine).

The days above were most certainly real and literal days in which specific things had to happen; they were not long, drawn-out periods of time. The text employs the use of ordinal numbers as does Genesis 1 but here we do not conclude that those days were indefinite periods of time; they were simply days. Thus even with ordinal numbers a *day* is just a literal, 24-hour day.

Days in Hosea 6:2

Certain Bible expositors have suggested that Hosea 6:2 uses *days* as ages of time (probably about one thousand years each) in relation to the nation of Israel and their national revival: "After two days He will revive us; on the third day He will raise us up, that we may live in His sight." While this is a provocative interpretation that cannot be disproved, the context does not demand such an interpretation and hence neither can it be positively proven. It could be that even here it is referring to two plus one literal days.

This survey of the usage of days in the Old Testament brings us back to the question of just how we are to understand the days of creation. We have seen that there are times when the word *day* is used for periods of time other than a literal 24-hour (though millions or billions of years are never implied). However, whenever a number is placed in front of the word *day*, the meaning becomes limited to that of a 24-hour period, that is, a regular day just as we use the word today to describe a day. Therefore, looking at Genesis 1, are we to interpret those days as literal, 24-hour days or long, indefinite periods of time in which evolution may have occurred?

The First Day

The glory of the Bible is that, unlike the writings of other ancient nations which demonstrated a belief that water was the primal material before the existence of any gods, it claims that God was in the beginning and that He created all that is. Both the Gap Theory and a relatively new theory, which posits that the six-day-creation-clock didn't really start ticking until God uttered the words "Let there be light" in verse 3, suggest that the first day didn't start in verse 1 but in either verse 2 or verse 3, respectively. Let us simply analyze, biblically and linguistically, the full range of the key Hebrew words in Genesis 1:1–2 and see what they mean and if they support the idea that a time gap exists in those verses. (English words for which the Hebrew equivalent is given are italicized.)

> In the beginning God *created* (ברא *bara*) *the heavens and the earth* (את השמים ואת הארץ *et hashayim ve'et ha'aretz*). The earth was without *form, and void* (תהו ובהו *tohu vavohu*); and darkness was on the face of the *deep*

(תהום *tehom*). And the Spirit of God was *hovering* (מרחפת *merachefet*) *over the face of the waters* (על־פני המים *al pnei hamayim*).

Bara and Asa

The first key word is ברא *created* (*bara*) which is used a total of fifty-three times in the Old Testament. The basic and majority times used form of the word, which is used in Genesis 1, has the general meaning of *create, shape,* or *form*. It has been suggested that the word *bara* used here in Genesis is a different type of action than the word עשה (*asa—do, make, fashion,* or *produce*) used in Exodus 20:11 where God says that He made the heavens and earth in six days.

Bara and *asa* are for the most part synonymous with one important distinction between them: *bara* is used only of God's actions and never of man's. There are countless examples of where man can *asa* (*do* or *make*); however, only God can *bara*. There is by implication creation *ex nihilo*, but the major thrust of the word *bara* lies in its use by God only and on the initiation of something new. The *Theological Wordbook of the Old Testament* (TWOT) notes concerning *asa* and its distinction from *bara*:

> The word [*asa*] occurs with great frequency in the Genesis account of creation, which is the first great act of God in history. The significant interchange between the words bara' "create" and 'asa is of great interest. The word bara' carries the thought of the initiation of the object involved. **It always connotes what only God can do and frequently emphasizes the absolute newness of the object created. The word 'asa is much broader in scope,** connoting primarily the fashioning of the object with little concern for special nuances.
>
> The use of bara' in the opening statement of the account of creation seems to carry the implication that the physical phenomena came into existence at that time and had no previous existence in the form in

which they were created by divine fiat. **The use of 'asa may simply connote the act of fashioning the objects involved in the whole creative process** (TWOT: 1708 *asa*).

As the TWOT notes, the use of *asa* is a broader term than *bara*, but we see from the context in which the words are used that they can be used interchangeably to a large extent. Perhaps the best example is Isaiah 45:18 where God is disparaging those who put their trust in idols rather than in Him, the true God and Creator of all. Notice that the three words used—*create, form,* and *make*—all describe the same event: the creation of the heavens and earth.

> For thus says the LORD,
> Who created (*bore* בורא) the heavens,
> Who is God,
> Who formed (*yotzer* יוצר) the earth and made (*oseh* עשה) it,
> Who has established it,
> Who did not create (*braha* בראה) it in vain,
> Who formed (*yatzarah* יצרה) it to be inhabited:
> "I am the LORD, and there is no other" (Isaiah 45:18).

This verse is incredibly specific, especially in regards to the creation of the earth. First of all, God declares that He is the one who created (*bore* בורא) the heavens—which could also be translated as *Creator of the heavens*. Next He says that He is the former (*yotzer* יוצר) and the maker (*oseh* עשה) of the earth, a seeming confirmation of the supposed distinction of *bara* and *asa*. However, God continues by saying that He created it, where the word *it*, is the third person singular feminine possessive suffix. Put simply, it means that the word *it* is attached to the word *created*. The word *it* must refer to *earth* because the *earth* is a singular feminine noun and *heavens* is a dual masculine noun. Clearly and unmistakably God declares that He created, formed, and made the earth. Thus, to suggest that Exodus 20:11 ("For in six days the LORD made [*asa*] the heavens and the earth, the sea, and all that is in them ...") is not parallel in thought to Genesis 1 is to ignore the evidence in favor of one's own theory.

The Heavens and Earth

Thus far verse 1 has told us the *when* of creation—in the beginning, and then the *how*—God created something completely new (*bara*), which only God can do. Now we are up to the *what*, which is of course: the heavens and the earth. The question before us is understanding what precisely that means since immediately in verse 2 we are told that the earth was formless and void (ובהו תהו *tohu vavohu*); the earth must have not been fully complete. Thus, just what did He create? What are we to understand by *the heavens and the earth*? Did He create them complete or could that term be understood as the material that He would later form, as if He first created the clay and then worked it into a suitable form?

The answer to this enigma lies in the fact that there is no single word for *universe* in Hebrew, which is confirmed by the *International Standard Bible Encyclopedia*, "The Hebrews had no proper word for 'world' in its wide sense of 'universe.' The nearest approach to such a meaning is in the phrase 'the heavens and the earth.'"[16] Thus, stating that God created *the heavens and the earth* is equivalent in our day to saying that He created the *universe*; it encompasses all that is.[17] Bible commentators Keil & Delitzsch note the significance of the first creative act found in the Bible:

> [...] there is nothing belonging to the composition of the universe, either in material or form, which had an existence out of God prior to this divine act in the beginning (Keil & Delitzsch Genesis 1:2).

That is to say, God essentially created the building blocks before beginning construction. The term *the heavens and the earth* here might be thought of as the raw material, the elements that God created out of nothing that He would form and fashion later to His liking. Consider that before God created anything, there was

language of Akkadian, which has a very similar meaning, thus helping us to better understand its use in the Bible:

> [...] [*tamtu*] is conceived in its primordial condition as [...] the primeval water as a sea, an ocean, before the earth was created by the heaping up of mud on the shore of this tamtu (Yahuda 1933: 128).

Physicist Dr. Russell Humphreys, in his book *Starlight and Time*, describes his theory based on the observations of this verse, how water might have then been transformed into the other known elements, "... this verse suggested to me that the original material God created, the deep, was pure water, which He then transformed into other materials"[22] (Humphreys 2004: 72).

Merachefet, God's Energizing of His Creation

> And the Spirit of God was *hovering* (מרחפת *merachefet*) *over the face of the waters* (על־פני המים *al panei hamayim*) (Genesis 1:2b).

The last word to analyze, מרחפת (*merachefet*), found also in Deuteronomy 32:11[23] denotes the fluttering, hovering, or brooding motion of a bird over its nest.

> As an eagle stirs up its nest,
> Hovers (מרחפת *merachefet*) over its young,
> Spreading out its wings, taking them up,
> Carrying them on its wings.

The purpose of the act of brooding by a bird over its nest is to provide warmth and nurturing to its young. The movement is that of the bird gently shaking and moving its body in fairly small motions. It also contains the idea of the bird covering its young with its wings, enveloping them in order to bring them to maturity.[24]

It seems that at this point God began to energize the raw material that He made in verse 1. The oscillation on the face (or surface) of the deep, which is really what the hovering could be compared to, created the movement of the inert elements. It is interesting that all matter and energy at their core are simply wavelengths: "matter acts as both a particle and as a wave" (Koehler 1996).

We saw above that the Hebrew letter *vav* attached to the front of the word *hayta* (*was*) created a type of parenthetical statement. The fact that מרחפת (*merachefet*) is a transitive participle substantiates that verse 2 is not a new thought or even the first act of God but a clarification of what came before it in verse 1.

God Speaks

The sequence of events is that the first thing God did was to create the heavens (space) and the earth (material)—that is, He created a place or dimension outside of Himself and then the matter to work with, which we are told was without form and empty. Then God, hovering over the face of the deep, decreed light to exist. These are the first recorded words of God, but in fact, the third creative act.

This view can be strongly defended from the Hebrew grammar. The typical sequence of a narrative is to start with a verb in the simple past tense[25] (Genesis 1:1 begins with *bara*—*created* in the simple past tense) thereby signifying something new or dramatic to the story. Verse 2, we saw, is a parenthetical statement explaining what is meant exactly by the creation of the "earth." The action picks up again in verse 3 with the use of a sequential past tense[26]. The use of a different kind of Hebrew verb marks quite clearly that the writer understood the actions of verse 3 to be a continuation of the previous two verses. Hebrew expert Dr. Buth notes that this is the normal storytelling construction in biblical Hebrew.

> The sequential past tense is used to present the next event in the story or the next event in a sentence. If the writer wants to mark a break in the flow of the story for any reason, then they do not use the sequential

past tense. For a past event they would need to put something other than the verb at the beginning of the sentence and then use a simple past tense (Buth 2005: 52).

Not only is verse 3 a continuation of verse 1, but the entire creation account of Genesis 1 uses the sequential past tense. Consequently, according to the grammar, there is no break between verse 1 and the rest of the chapter.

Thus, there is no reason to try to place millions of years between any of the first three verses since they are all part of that first day. Light was created on the first day, along with the very building blocks necessary for even the light to shine, which was energized by the movement of the Holy Spirit over the face of the deep. There exists, therefore, no reason to believe that the length of the first day was any different than that of any other, nor was there a previous world that fell only to be recreated, nor was there even a geologic creation some billions of years earlier. The first three verses of Genesis 1, the first day, all occurred within 24 hours just like the rest of the days as we shall see.

The Days in Genesis 1

The days in Genesis 1 should certainly be understood as literal, 24-hour days due to the usage of the limitation of *the evening and the morning*[27] found throughout Genesis 1 (the fact that the sun was not created until the fourth day is irrelevant since the rotation of the earth is what constitutes a day—the light source is immaterial). Even though the evidence seems to point to literal, 24-hour days in Genesis 1, the old-earth camp is still persuaded that these days are long periods of time rather than normal (24-hour) days. They suggest that the usage of ordinal numbers (first, second, third, fourth, etc.) rather than cardinals, as noted previously, denotes different eras of time; thus the *first* era (day) is followed by the *second* era (day), etc. where each day equals an unknown but extremely long period of time in which the slow processes of evolution, with God's help, had enough time, according to Darwin's model of slow change.

There are some fatal flaws to this theory, however, from a biblical perspective. First of all, the first day of Genesis in the Hebrew is not actually defined as the first day, but rather as *day one* or *yom echad* יום אחד. The word *echad* is the cardinal number *one* and should not be understood as first ראשון *rishon*, but as in the series *one, two, three, four, etc.* We have seen previously that any time *day* occurs with a cardinal number, it always refers to a literal, 24-hour day. So we can conclude that the first day of creation was 24 hours.

God Defines the Days for Us

The absolute solution to this puzzle of the length of the days in Genesis is given by God Himself. After taking the children of Israel out of Egypt, God led them to a place called Mount Sinai where He gave them the Law. In Exodus chapter 20, verses 9 and 10, God states,

> "Six days you shall labor and do all your work, but the seventh day is the Sabbath of the LORD your God. In it you shall do no work: you, nor your son, nor your daughter, nor your male servant, nor your female servant, nor your cattle, nor your stranger who is within your gates."

There is no doubt whatsoever that God is talking about a regular workweek. The people were to work six (literal) days and then they were to take a day off, something very different from the custom of the peoples around them, who generally didn't take any days off.

In verse 11 of chapter 20 God gives the reason and history behind the seven-day week:

> For in six days the LORD made the heavens and the earth, the sea, and all that is in them, and rested the

seventh day. Therefore the LORD blessed the Sabbath
day and hallowed it.

Here God unequivocally declares that He created everything
in only six days. As with the other times that a cardinal number
appears before the word *day* (*yom* יום), here too it is used as a
literal, 24-hour day. So God makes perfectly clear how long He
took to make the universe (just in case anyone should be confused). If these days are not taken as literal days then neither can
the Sabbath be taken as literal. However, the fact that the Sabbath
is a literal day starting at sunset Friday evening and lasting until
the following Saturday evening goes back in Hebrew tradition
as far back as Mount Sinai and is a very cherished day. Since we
know that the Sabbath has always been considered a literal span
of 24 hours, we can safely conclude that the six days of creation
are to be taken literally as well.

It would seem that God wanted to reiterate[28] the message for
those that still didn't get it. In Exodus 31:15, 17, He says,

> "Work shall be done for six days, but the seventh is
> the Sabbath of rest, holy to the LORD. Whoever does
> any work on the Sabbath day, he shall surely be put
> to death [...] It is a sign between Me and the children
> of Israel forever; for in six days the LORD made the
> heavens and the earth, and on the seventh day He
> rested and was refreshed."

There is no way to circumvent this declaration: the Sabbath,
the day of rest, the seventh day of the week, observed for 24-
hours every week, is a sign between the Jewish people and
God. Transgressing the covenant was punishable by death. The
Israelites knew exactly how long it was—for not knowing would
cost them their life. The Sabbath was/is 24 hours and, therefore,
so are all of the other days of the week, which is how long it took
God to create the heavens and the earth. This is a far cry from an
indefinite period of time.

The Days in Genesis 2

The claim is often made that the creation accounts of Genesis 1 (really 1:1–2:3) and Genesis 2 (really 2:4–2:25) are contradictory. Thus, it is suggested that even if chapter 1 had been written with a literal intent, chapter 2, and its contradictions to chapter 1, renders a literal reading impossible. The principal difference in the two chapters is that chapter 1 deals with creation from a panoramic view while chapter 2 is concerned specifically with the *how* of the creation of man and the *what* of man's role in God's creation. The key passages that we need to consider are 2:4, 2:5–7, and 2:19. Once we understand these correctly, the entire chapter neatly fits with chapter 1.

Genesis 2:4

It has been suggested that Genesis 2:4 supports the theory that the days of the Genesis creation account long vast ages. The verse reads:

> This is the history of the heavens and the earth when they were created, in the day that the LORD God made the earth and the heavens.

Progressive Creation advocate Hugh Ross states concerning this verse,

> This verse, a summary statement for the creation account, in the literal Hebrew reads, "These are the generations of the heavens and the earth when they were created in the day of their making. ..." Here, the word *day* refers to all six-creation days (and the creation events prior to the first creative day). Obviously, then, it refers to a period longer than 24 hours. Hebrew lexicons verify that the word for *generation* (*toledah*) refers to the time it takes a baby to become a parent or to a time period arbitrarily longer. In Genesis 2:4 the plural form, *generations*, is used, indicating that multiple generations have passed (Ross 1991: 52).

Ross here asserts things about Hebrew that are not accurate. The problem with getting the literal reading of a passage with the aid of lexicons is that the idioms as defined by the context are often overlooked. Consider for example the English word *bow*—this could mean many different things depending on its context. One meaning is a weapon, another is the front of a ship, still another is the decoration on a gift, and the fourth is to bend at the waist. Not only are the definitions radically different, but it can also be used as a noun and as a verb. Without context we don't know what it means nor can we even pronounce it correctly!

Dr. Ross has failed to recognize the idiom behind the words *in the day (that the LORD God) made*. The Hebrew expression ביום עשות (*b'yom asot*) actually carries the force of *when*. The letter ב (*beth*) in Hebrew often designates a temporal aspect. Joüon & Muraoka note in *A Grammar of Biblical Hebrew*, "With the infinitive ב is used in the temporal sense." This explains why the letter *beth* in בהבראם (*b'hibaram*) is translated **when they were created**, a fact also supported by both the *Brown Driver Briggs Lexicon*, and *Gesenius' Hebrew Grammar*[29]. *B'yom* is part of a three-word construct chain and it is used in relation to the infinitive *asot* (*making*) which again carries the force of *when*. What is important not to overlook here, however, is that when *yom* is used in conjunction with the preposition *beth* it may be understood as a less precise expression than the 24-hour day.[30] When *yom* is used with a number, it always refers to a literal, 24-hour day.

Ross also misunderstands the full range of meaning of the word תולדות (*toledoth*), which often means *generations*, but is in many places better translated as *account* or *history*.[31] Thus, owning a Hebrew lexicon is not enough to fully capture the nuances of the language.

Genesis 2:5–2:7

> [...] before any plant of the field was in the earth and before any herb of the field had grown. For the LORD God had not caused it to rain on the earth, and there was no man to till the ground; but a mist went up from

the earth and watered the whole face of the ground. And the LORD God formed man of the dust of the ground, and breathed into his nostrils the breath of life; and man became a living being.

A casual reading of 2:5 to 2:7 in English would seem to indicate that man was created before plants and shrubs. The question that we must consider is exactly which plants and shrubs. Is this referring to all of the vegetation on the entire planet or is it more defined? The vegetation referred to is designated by the word *field*, which appears twice in the text. שיח השדה (*siach hasadeh*) *plant of the field* and עשב השדה (*esev hasadeh*) *herb of the field* are the technical terms that we must not overlook. Both of them are in the construct state, which simply means that two nouns are considered one unit. It is very similar in English where *bicycle tire* is not referring to *bicycle* and *tire*, but a type of tire, that is, the *tire of a bicycle*. So too, we could just as well translate these as *field plant* and *field herb*—two specific items. Reputed Bible commentators Keil & Delitzsch note,

> The creation of the plants is not alluded to here at all, but simply the planting of the garden in Eden. The growing of the shrubs and sprouting of the herbs is different from the creation or first production of the vegetable kingdom, and relates to the growing and sprouting of the plants and germs which were called into existence by the creation, the natural development of the plants as it had steadily proceeded ever since the creation. This was dependent upon rain and human culture; their creation was not. Moreover, *the shrub and herb of the field* do not embrace the whole of the vegetable productions of the earth. It is not a fact that *the field* is used in the second section in the same sense as the earth in the first. שדה [*sadeh*] is not 'the widespread plain of the earth, the broad expanse of land,' but a field of arable land, soil fit for cultivation, which forms only a part of the "earth" or "ground" Keil & Delitzsch 1866: Genesis 2:5–2:7).

Genesis 2:19

> Out of the ground the LORD God formed every beast
> of the field and every bird of the air, and brought them
> to Adam to see what he would call them. And what-
> ever Adam called each living creature, that was its
> name.

Here too there is considered to be a contradiction to the first chapter since it would seem that God first formed Adam and then the animals. The word *formed* is the Hebrew word ויצר (*vay-itzer*) and is in the past tense. This form, however, can potentially express a simple past tense and the past of the past, known grammatically as the past perfect[32]. The past perfect is used to express any action that happened prior to another, both occurring in the past. For example, Johnny *had eaten* three hamburgers before he ordered dessert. The past perfect, *had eaten*, was finished before the action of *ordering*.

Thus the word *vayitzer* can signify either the simple past or past perfect. What that means practically is that *formed* could just as well have been translated as *had formed*.[33] The Hebrew supports either which would then yield a plausible translation, "Out of the ground the LORD God **had** formed every beast of the field and every bird of the air, and brought them to Adam ..." The use of the past perfect here, grammatically speaking, clears up the order of creation events perfectly: God first created the animals, then created man, and then brought the animals that He had created to man to see what he would call them (on day six).

A Final Objection

In Peter's second letter, he writes to fellow believers who were suffering all kinds of trials and persecutions on account of their belief in Jesus. His words are to comfort them and remind them that God's perspective is different from ours. He writes, "But, beloved, do not forget this one thing, that with the Lord one day is as a thousand years, and a thousand years as one day"

(2 Peter 3:8). This verse has been used to supposedly prove that time and numbers in the Bible do not have concrete value and therefore the *days* in Genesis 1 could have lasted one thousand years or perhaps even one million. But is Peter really saying that one day is equal to one thousand years? Looking at the verse again carefully we note that there are two important keys to a correct understanding.

With the Lord

The first key is "with the Lord." Peter here is describing God's perspective to time and not man's. This cannot be overlooked. Peter is not saying that one thousand years is equal to one day. He is saying that in God's economy, time is radically different and that when we think that the Lord is "slack" we should think again. "The Lord is not slack concerning His promise, as some count slackness, but is longsuffering toward us, not willing that any should perish but that all should come to repentance" (2 Peter 3:9). Peter wants to make clear that God's timetable is different from ours.

A Little Word with Big Meaning

The other important key is the little word *as* (*hos*) ὡς. Although small, it plays an important function in that it tells us that two things are similar but not exact in nature. It is no different than when we make such statements as "Johnny is like his father" or "In Johnny's eyes, his father is as Hercules." Both statements are merely stating that one is like or similar to another but not the same as the other. So too, Peter is saying that in the eyes of God, a day is similar to one thousand years and vice versa, one thousand years is like a day. This verse simply confirms that God is not bound by time. Peter gives us another example of the use of this little word in his first epistle where he says, "All flesh is as grass, and all the glory of man as the flower of the grass" (1 Peter 1:24). Certainly, he is not saying we are actually grass growing on the field. He merely says that we are in many ways similar to grass. Just as grass has a short life, so too are our lives short when compared with the eternal God and so too will our glory fade away faster than we think. Thus, to God a day and a thousand years are the same.

Psalm 90:4

This truth was first stated in the Old Testament, which Peter more than likely drew from: "For a thousand years in Your sight are like yesterday when it is past, and like a watch in the night" (Psalm 90:4). Here too, the writer is simply stating things from God's point of view—that is, time has no bearing on God. He is not bound by time and hence whether it is a day or one thousand years, it is the same to Him. We are not to conclude, however, that time is irrelevant for us. Again and again, we see that people in the Bible lived real lives for a specific amount of time. The Bible treats the lifespan of the lives of Adam (930 years), Noah (950 years), Abraham (175 years), Sarah (127 years), Jacob (147 years), and Moses (120 years) as all real and definite (see Genesis 5:5, 9:29, 25:7, 23:1, 47:28, and Deuteronomy 34:7, respectively). Notice that Adam and Noah lived close to one thousand years. Their lifetime was like a single day in the eyes of the Lord, but nevertheless, they lived a specific number of years. Jacob, in giving an overview of his years, in no way intimated that they passed by as if they were just a day:

> "And Jacob said to Pharaoh, 'The days of the years of my pilgrimage are one hundred and thirty years; few and evil have been the days of the years of my life, and they have not attained to the days of the years of the life of my fathers in the days of their pilgrimage'" (Genesis 47:9).

Summary of the Days in Genesis 1 and 2

In summary, we have seen that sometimes the word *day* (*yom* יוֹם) carries a meaning of more than just a 24-hour period. However, every time the word is used in conjunction with a cardinal or ordinal number, the meaning is always and without exception limited to the period of a regular and literal day—that is, a period of 24 hours. God Himself reiterates that He created the heavens and the earth in six days, which is why He instructs man to work six days and then to take the seventh off. We know from history that the Hebrews have always taken the six-day workweek literally and have considered the seventh day to be a day of rest. Because God tells us twice in Exodus (20:11 and 31:17) that those were literal days, our only plausible conclusion regarding the six (plus one) days in Genesis is that they are to be taken as literal, 24-hour days. We need not and cannot conclude that they were six indefinite periods of time, at least not if we are to take everything else in the Bible seriously.

The only reason to conclude that the six days of creation were long periods of time is if we seek to harmonize the Bible with the model of (geological, chemical, and biological) evolution. However, if we simply seek to allow Scripture to interpret Scripture, then the interpretation of Genesis 1 is clear: God created the heavens and the earth in six literal, 24-hour days and rested on the seventh. We therefore conclude from biblical evidence that God made the heavens and the earth in six literal days. There is no room for a biblical interpretation which includes an evolutionary process of billions of years during creation; God emphatically declares to have done it in six literal days.

6-"Days" According to Ancient Jewish Commentators

> Accordingly Moses says, That in just six days the
> world, and all that is therein, was made (Josephus
> *Antiquities* Book 1, Chapter 1).

We now turn our attention to discover what the ancient Bible
commentators understood those six days to mean when they
opened up to Genesis 1 and 2. Did they see extremely long indefinite periods of time? Or did they see regular, 24-hour days?
Would they come to the same conclusion that we have reached?
Or would they be inclined to look for a deeper, hidden meaning
in the text? Even if it can be demonstrated that all or nearly all of
the ancient interpreters thought that the Bible and Genesis 1 in
particular should be interpreted as six literal days, that does not
prove that that is in fact the reality of the Bible. However, if the
overwhelming majority understood the creation account to be
referring to a week of six literal days, then it would greatly support our previous conclusion and prove that the normal method
of interpretation or hermeneutic of Scripture was to take it at
face value.

We will see that when we examine the ancient Jewish and

Christian commentators on what they believed concerning the beginning of the world, they almost always talk about the end of it as well. They claim that the age of the earth is less than six thousand years old. This becomes an important control for us in that by claiming that the earth was created less than six thousand years previous to their day, they are stating their belief in a young earth, and hence, the six literal 24-hour days of creation.

The Use of Ancient Interpreters

The point of view of ancient interpreters and commentators is very relevant to us because we know that they were in no way influenced by the teachings of Darwinian evolution, which requires billions of years to occur. The ancient perspective has already been exploited by those seeking to establish that Scripture actually teaches that the earth and the universe are incredibly old. Perhaps the most prominent of the Progressive Creation perspective is Dr. Hugh Ross. While we do not wish to question his sincerity nor his belief in the God of the Bible, his interpretation of these ancient commentators is in need of serious review. Ross states in his book *The Fingerprint of God*:

> Many of the early Church Fathers and other biblical scholars interpret the creation days of Genesis 1 as long periods of time. The list includes the Jewish historian Josephus (1st century); Irenaeus, bishop of Lyons, apologist and martyr (2nd century); Origen, who rebutted heathen attacks on Christian doctrine (3rd century); Basil (4th century); Augustine (5th century); and, later, Aquinas (13th century), to name a few. The significance of this list lies not only in the prominence of these individuals as biblical scholars, defenders of the faith, and pillars of the early church (except Josephus), but also in that their scriptural views cannot be said to have been shaped to accommodate secular opinion. Astronomical, paleontological, and geological evidences for the antiquity of the

universe, of the earth, and of life did not come forth until the nineteenth century (Ross 1991: 141).

Ross's list of ancient biblical scholars is at first impressive. But when we begin to study his sources in depth, we find that, at the very least, Ross has not been diligent in his investigation. Reality is simply not as he states it. The claim that many of these ancient interpreters believed the creation days to be longer than 24 hours is later parroted by an advocate of Progressive Creation who states:

> Dr. Hugh Ross documents in detail what first century Jewish scholars and the early Christian Church Fathers said regarding their interpretation of creation chronology (see Chapter 2, pages 16–24). Many early Church Fathers expressed no opinion on the subject of creation days, since it is a peripheral issue in Christianity. However, Jewish scholars who discussed creation chronology include Philo and Josephus, while Christian fathers include Justin Martyr, Irenaeus, Hippolytus (through writings of Ambrose), Clement, Origen, Lactantius, Victorinus, Methodius, Augustine, Eusebius, Basil, and Ambrose. Among this group, all but one believed that the creation days were longer than 24 hours. The evidence presented in *Creation and Time* is both overwhelming and well documented (all references are given) (Deem 2006a).

Again, we are not questioning whether Dr. Ross and others of the Progressive Creation position are sincere and hold the God of the Bible in high esteem. It is their scholarship that is in question. The truth is that many, if not almost all, of the early Church Fathers (ante-Nicene) definitively thought that the universe was made in six literal days. Additionally, most ancient Jewish commentators shared the same point of view—namely, that the heavens and earth were created in six literal days. Let's examine the evidence to see what those interpreters thought about the time frame of creation. Did they hold to a literal, straightforward, six-day creation as we claim that the Bible teaches? Or did they believe that allegorizing the text was the proper method of interpretation?

Targumim

A very important source to consider when addressing the issue of how ancient interpreters understood the Bible are the Targumim. Targumim (*Targum* is singular) are the Aramaic translations of the Old Testament Scriptures. They were for the most part written both in and outside of Israel a few centuries after the time of Jesus. They were written either for those Jews who had lost Hebrew as their mother tongue because of living outside of Israel for so long or for those living in Israel after the time of the Second Jewish Revolt (135 AD) when Hebrew truly started to die out.[34] Those Jews were no longer comfortable reading the Scriptures solely in Hebrew, but needed the help of a translation as they read along in the original Hebrew. However, the Targumim were much more than merely word-for-word translations. They were running commentaries on the Scriptures filled with typical Jewish interpretations. The Hebrew text of the Bible was always considered sacred by the Jews, and therefore, it was to be approached with great care. The text was never to be touched. Because the Targumim were in Aramaic and not Hebrew, there was no risk that the commentaries might be mistaken for the actual words of the Bible itself.

Targum Onkelos

Targum Onkelos translates Genesis 1:1 very literally: "In the first times the Lord created the heavens and the earth. And the earth was waste and empty, and darkness was upon the face of the abyss." In fact, the entire chapter of Targum Onkelos of Genesis 1 shows no indication whatsoever that the translator/commentator was persuaded that the six days of Genesis were to be taken in any way but literally. Conversely, the translator actually places a comment in chapter 3 regarding the curse put on the Serpent and the promised Savior.

> And I will put enmity between thee and between the woman, and between thy son and her son. He will remember thee, what thou didst to him (at) **from the beginning**, and thou shalt be observant unto him at the end (emphasis mine).

Notice that here the Targumist defines when the time of this occurred—"from the beginning." Although this doesn't prove that the six days in Genesis were truly literal, it does demonstrate that an ancient interpreter *understood* them as being literal since the time of the fall happened in the beginning, not some millions or billions of years after the initial act of creation.

Targum Jonathan

Targum Jonathan[35], in translating Genesis 2:3 (which is really the end of chapter 1 and is an unfortunate and mistaken chapter break), adds a reason which goes beyond the original text by adding the words "the days of the week."

> And the creatures of the heavens and earth, and all the hosts of them, were completed. And the Lord had finished by the Seventh Day the work which He had wrought, [...] And the Lord blessed the Seventh Day more than all the **days of the week**, and sanctified it, because in it He rested from all His works which the Lord had created and had willed to make (emphasis mine).

The words "the days of the week" demonstrate that the Targumist also understood the first through sixth days in Genesis 1 to be "the days of the week" and the seventh to be the final day of that week. What did he have in mind when he added that comment that is not found in the Hebrew Scriptures? Did his belief that the seventh was blessed more than all the other days of the week actually mean that the last age or era of time was better than the rest? Or did he think that days of the week meant *Sunday, Monday, Tuesday*, etc. (or as it would be in Hebrew *First Day, Second Day, Third Day*, etc.)? If we consider what God declared to Moses via the Targumim as we did in the Hebrew Bible, then the conclusion of six literal days becomes very difficult to circumvent.

> For in six days the Lord created the heavens, and the earth, and the sea, and whatever is therein, and rested on the seventh day: therefore the Lord hath blessed the day of Shabbatha and sanctified it (Targum Jonathan, Exodus 20:11).

This is again reiterated in the same Targum in Exodus 31:15 and 17:

> Six days ye shall do work; but the seventh day is Sabbath, the holy Sabbath before the Lord [...] **For in six days the Lord created and perfected the heavens and the earth; and in the seventh day He rested and refreshed** (emphasis mine).

The Targum of Onkelos confirms again that the commonly accepted time frame for the creation of the heavens and the earth was but a mere six literal days. There is no intimation that those days somehow really meant long, indefinite ages of perhaps billions of years.

> **For in six days the Lord made the heavens and the earth, the seas and all that is in them,** and rested on the seventh day; wherefore the Lord blessed the day of Shabbatha, and sanctified it (Targum Onkelos, Exodus 20:11, emphasis mine).
>
> **Six days** shalt thou do work, and the seventh day is Sabbath, the Holy Sabbath before the Lord [...] for in **six days the Lord made the heavens and the earth**; and in the seventh day rested and was refreshed (Targum Onkelos Exodus 31: 15, 17, emphasis mine).

These passages are some of the clearest passages in the Bible regarding the time God took to create everything and yet there isn't even a minor hint that those time frames mean anything other than what we can take at face value. Although the Targumim are not listed among the ancient Jewish writers cited by Dr. Ross and others, they are certainly an important source, and one of the primary sources when wanting to know about common Jewish thought just before and after the time of Christ.

Josephus

An indispensable voice of Jewish history and thought in first century Israel is that of Josephus, who appears on the list of supposed ancient supporters of an old earth. Josephus is considered the most important source historians have regarding the events of the destruction of the Jewish Temple in Jerusalem in 70 AD. Josephus single-handedly wrote the history of the debacle of the Jewish state at the hands of their Roman enemies. Born in 37 AD, Josephus was raised a Jew in Israel and fought alongside his Jewish countrymen before being taken a hostage by the Romans, who granted him the opportunity to write not only the story of the *Wars of the Jews*, but also later a work entitled *The Antiquities of the Jews*. Josephus' mother tongue was Hebrew. His expertise in Hebrew and the fact that he was also well-acquainted with the Hebrew Scriptures were essential in writing *Antiquities of the Jews*. While not everything that Josephus wrote is considered to always be accurate or without bias, recent discoveries in the past one hundred years have proven that Josephus's account of Jewish history was extremely accurate.[36]

From the Creation

Josephus opens his monumental work *Antiquities of the Jews* with a rather significant chapter title: "Containing the Interval of Three Thousand Eight Hundred and Thirty-Three Years. From the Creation to the Death of Isaac." Just from the chapter title one already begins to see that Josephus understood the time from the creation until the death of Isaac as a relatively short period— 3,833 years. Adding that to the time from Isaac (approximately 1950 BC) to the time of Josephus (about 80 AD) we get a number of 5,863 years—hardly millions of years. There is absolutely no suggestion from him that "the creation" happened indefinite ages ago; rather it was but a relatively short time ago. It is interesting that Josephus' date corresponds very closely with that of young earth creationists' calculations based on the genealogies of the Bible. The point is that Josephus in no way thought that the days of creation were long periods of millions or billions of years. He then begins with the same words as found directly in the Bible, "In the beginning God created the heavens and the earth." He goes on:

> God commanded that there should be light: and when that was made, he considered the whole mass, and separated the light and the darkness; and the name he gave to one was *Night,* and the other he called *Day:* and he named the beginning of light, and the time of rest, *The Evening* and *The Morning,* and this was indeed the first day. But Moses said it was one day. Accordingly Moses says, **That in just six days the world,** and all that is therein, **was made.** And that the seventh day was a rest, and a release from the labor of such operations; whence it is that we celebrate a rest from our labors on that day, and call it the Sabbath, which word denotes *rest* in the Hebrew tongue (Josephus *Antiquities* Book 1, Chapter 1, emphasis mine).

Notice that Josephus is careful to note that there was evening and there was morning, which he says was the first day, but then he adds "But Moses said it was one day." By doing this, he not only demonstrates his understanding of Hebrew, but also points out that the Hebrew shows that all of these events happened in one day. He also states his opinion since it is not directly in the text of Genesis 1, though, it is more than likely that he was merely parroting the commonly accepted belief.

In Just Six Days

Josephus in no way thought that the days of creation were long periods of time in which the slow process of evolution happened! He says that "in just six days the world *and all that is therein*" was made. He then discusses that the origin of the Jews resting on the seventh day came from God resting on the seventh day. Keep in mind that Josephus has to explain the history of his people to Romans who would probably have known next to nothing about the religion of one of the people in their vast empire. The most that they might have known was that his people foolishly rebelled against them and consequently paid the price for their rebellion. So Josephus has to explain the small details in order for them to truly appreciate the splendor of the Jewish sacred book.

Here too, we find that one of the most prominent ancient commentators thought nothing but of a literal, six-day creation. The thought of a day of the creation week equaling millions or billions of years or even some super long duration just never crossed his mind. Conversely, he clearly states that in just six days God made all that is.

Rabbinic Interpretation

We next turn to rabbinic interpretation in hopes of discovering what they thought about the six days of creation. Did they too interpret the days of Genesis 1 to be literal days of 24-hours like those that we have already seen, or as it has been suggested, did they allegorize those as days of incredibly long duration? We should note that rabbinic interpretation of the Scriptures is such that it generally seeks to find a deeper meaning to the text. They quite often would take what would seem to us to be two rather dissimilar passages, and through a few keys words, tie them together in such a way as to teach a deeper truth.

For example, let's look at tractate Sabbath 17, Chapter 7 which, as the title suggests, deals with the Sabbath and the regulations necessary to properly keep it. The rabbis are discussing what to do if someone who is traveling misses the Sabbath due to not knowing which day it is.

> R. Huna said: One who has been traveling in a desert and does not know what day is Sabbath, must count six days from the day (on which he realizes) that he has missed the Sabbath, and observe the seventh. Hyya b. Rabh said: He must observe that very day and then continue his counting from that day. And what is the point of their differing? The former holds that one must act in accordance with the **creation (which commenced six days before the Sabbath), while the latter holds that one must be guided by Adam's creation (on the eve of Sabbath)** (emphasis mine).

The rabbis immediately turn to the week of creation as a real week whereby they might demonstrate how one must count the days before the Sabbath. They then look back at the creation week from the point of view that Adam was made on the eve of the Sabbath, which was the literal sixth day of time. Thus, the days of a workweek plus the Sabbath are equal to the days of the creation week.

The Talmud Comments on the Mishna

The Talmud comments on the discussion in the Mishna[37] concerning one who might ask "what was before creation?" and tries to draw out further applications and to answer any questions unresolved.

> Lest one assume that a man can ask, **What was before the creation**? therefore it is written: "**Since the day that God created man from the earth**"; but lest one assume, a man must not ask even what was done in the **six days of creation**? (*Book 3 Tract Hagigah 4 chapter 2*).

Notice that they make reference to the six days of creation and very matter-of-factly state "what was done in the six days of creation." The implication is that those days were real days, not long, drawn-out, indefinite ages.

Rashi

From another portion of the Talmud we read:

> Four thousand two hundred and thirty-one years after
> the creation of the world, if any one offers thee for one
> single denarius a field worth a thousand denarii, do
> not buy it (*Avodah Zarah*, fol. 9, col. 2).

According to this passage the creation of the world happened
4,231 years previous to the statement. The famed medieval
Jewish commentator Rashi (below) was noted to have given
an explanation on the passage that helps us understand what
ancient Jews believed concerning the time that elapsed from creation until their time.

> Rashi gives this as the reason of the prohibition: For
> then the restoration of the Jews to their own land will
> take place, so that the denarius paid for a field in a for-
> eign land would be money thrown away. **Four thou-
> sand two hundred and ninety-one years after the
> creation of the world** the wars of the dragons and the
> wars of Gog and Magog will cease, **and the rest of the
> time will be the days of the Messiah;** and **the Holy
> One—blessed be He!—will not renew His world
> till after seven thousand years** ... Rabbi Jonathan
> said, "May the bones of those who compute the latter
> days (when the Messiah shall appear) be blown; for
> some say, 'Because the time (of Messiah) has come and
> Himself has not, therefore He will never come!' But
> wait thou for Him, as it is said (Hab. ii. 3), 'Though He
> tarry, wait for Him'" (*Sanhedrin*, fol. 97, col. 2, empha-
> sis mine).

Rashi evidently separated human history, *from the time of creation* until the end, into seven thousand years. Notice that Rashi
understood these years as real periods of time that began *in the
beginning* with the creation of the world. This fact is further established by Rabbi Jonathan by noting it is not good to compute the

time of the Messiah, which, according to some Jews, had already come. For a Christian, this is a very significant statement, but to pursue it would derail us from our current discussion that key, ancient rabbis understood the earth to be young—less than six thousand years.

Other Rabbis

A few other examples only serve to confirm what we have seen so far—namely, that ancient rabbis considered the creation week to be nothing less than real days and not day-ages as is often suggested. The *Rabba* commentaries (Harris, Translator 1901) on the Bible yield several important perspectives on the literalness of the six-day creation. The first chapter of *Genesis Rabba* asserts "Even the new heavens and earth, spoken of by the Prophet Isaiah (65:17), were created in the six days of creation." Another discussion from the Talmud regarding the importance of the Hebrew month Tishri states it this way, "Rabbi Eleazer said [...] On the first of *Tishri* Adam was created; from his existence we count our years, that is the **sixth day of the creation**" (*Talmud* Part 5, Holy Days, emphasis mine). Exodus Rabba 23 associates the formation of Adam with the event of creation itself,

> The song of praise that Israel offered on the Red Sea was pleasing to God as an outburst of real gratitude. There had indeed been no such praise offered to God since creation. Adam, formed out of dust and put above all creation, omitted to praise the Creator for the dignity conferred on him (Exodus Rabba 23).

Leviticus Rabba 14 succinctly places man along with the creation, "Man is the last in **creation** and the first in responsibility." If God started making the universe some fifteen billion years earlier, it would be hard to link man with creation due to the enormous time gap between them. Midrash Esther 1 offers a similar scenario,

> As early as the time of creation it was decreed that the following should have precedence, each in his own

sphere. Adam was first of man, Cain of murderers, and Abel of the murdered. Noah the first to escape from peril (Harris, Translator 1901).

And finally, another rabbinic source, *Tanchum Bereshith* unequivocally states that God created in six days,

> As one who finishes the building of his house proclaims that day a holiday, and consecrates the building, so God, having finished creation in the six days, proclaimed the seventh day a holy day and sanctified it (electronic version, The Word Bible Software).

Where is the slightest hint in any of the aforementioned sources that they believed in an old earth and universe? Where does one get the impression that the ancient rabbis truly believed that God did not actually create in six literal days but in six day-ages each lasting some billions of years? Those day-ages are conspicuously missing. They only show up if one's theory depends on such interpretations. Even Philo, the very allegorical Jewish philosopher of first century Alexandria, Egypt, thought that the days of creation as recorded in Genesis were referring to six literal days.

Philo

If there were someone that we should expect to back up the old-earth theory, it would be Philo. Philo was an Alexandrian Jew who was born approximately twenty years before Jesus. Philo knew the Hebrew Scriptures very well and was very fond of them. However, he also was open to the ideas of Greek philosophy and tried to marry the two to accommodate both worldviews. The *International Standard Bible Encyclopedia* (ISBE) states concerning Philo:

> He addressed himself to two tasks, difficult to weld into a flawless unity. On the one hand, he wrote for educated men in Greek-Roman society, attempting to

explain, often to justify, his racial religion before them
[...] On the other hand, he had to confront his orthodox coreligionists, with their separatist traditions and
their contempt for paganism in all its works. He tried
to persuade them that, after all, Greek thought was
not inimical to their cherished doctrines, but, on the
contrary, involved similar, almost identical, principles
(ISBE: *Philo*, point 3).

The ISBE continues by saying that Philo represented a position
which tried to blend the philosophy of Hellenism with the "historical and dogmatic deductions of the Jewish Scriptures" (ISBE:
Philo, point 3), which resulted in rather strange interpretations.
Furthermore the ISBE states:

He taught that the Scriptures contain two meanings:
a "lower" meaning, obvious in the literal statements
of the text; and a "higher," or hidden meaning, per-
ceptible to the "initiate" alone. In this way he found it
possible to reconcile Greek intellectualism with Jewish
belief. Greek thought exhibits the "hidden" meaning; it turns out to be the elucidation of the "allegory"
which runs through the Old Testament like a vein of
gold (ISBE: *Philo*, point 3).

Thus, even if we were to find an allegorical meaning associated with the creation of the world in his writings, we would
understand that the allegorical side was Philo's attempt to reconcile the historical text of the Bible with the philosophy of Greek
thought. Therefore such an allegory would not be indicative of
the true meaning of the biblical text. What we actually see Philo
say regarding the creation, both from a literal and allegorical
point of view, is astonishing.

Philo's Paraphrase

Philo begins his treatise with the creation of the world as
given by Moses. That is to say, Philo is loosely paraphrasing the
Genesis account in his own words. This is extremely important

to note since here we have a writer that is very much in favor of interpreting Scripture from an allegorical approach and yet he lets us know what he thought Moses was truly communicating before moving on to his allegorical method.

> And he says that **the world was made in six days, not because the Creator stood in need of a length of time** (for it is natural that God should do everything at once, not merely by uttering a command, but by even thinking of it); but because **the things created required arrangement**; and number is akin to arrangement; and, of all numbers, six is, by the laws of nature, the most productive ... (Philo, *On The Creation* - Part 1 III. 13).

Philo is actually saying here that the world was made in six days which was actually much more time than God required. He says that God took His time "because the things created required arrangement." According to Philo, God slowed Himself down not for His own sake since merely by thinking He could have made all, but so that there would be order. The old-earth position is right in suggesting that God *could* have taken billions of years to create the world. But they miss the mark when affirming that God actually *did*. According to Scripture and all of the testimony we have seen up until now, God did go at an incredibly slow pace—that is if you are God! The passing of a mere thought versus creating at a tremendously slow speed of six (24-hour) days are radically different. Rather than confirming the old-earth position as Dr. Ross has suggested, Philo defends the belief that the biblical creation occurred in just a six-day week.

Philo's Allegorical Treatise

After providing his paraphrase of Genesis 1, Philo next begins his allegorical treatise to pull out the deeper truths and thereby make the Bible more palatable to his Greco-Roman audience:

> "And the heaven and the earth and all their world was completed." [Genesis 2:1] Having previously related

the creation of the mind and of sense, Moses now pro-
ceeds to describe the perfection which was brought
about by them both. And he says that neither the indi-
visible mind nor the particular sensations received
perfection, but only ideas, one the idea of the mind,
the other of sensation. And, speaking symbolically,
he calls the mind heaven, since the natures which can
only be comprehended by the intellect are in heaven.
And sensation he calls earth, because it is sensation
which has obtained a corporeal and some what earthy
constitution (Philo, *Allegorical Interpretation*, I - Part 1).

It is obvious that Philo is now speaking in a very allegorical
fashion. However, if we read carefully the above paragraph, we
see that in his allegorizing of Genesis 1 he is rejecting altogether
that Moses is referring to any type of numerical value of the creation regardless of how long that might have taken. He is advocating, allegorically speaking, neither a literal six-day creation
nor a six day-age theory. The amount of time required is absolutely inconsequential to him. Notice below in his statement that
time is not the issue.

"And on the sixth day God finished his work which
he had made." It would be a sign of great simplicity to
think that the world was created in six days, or **indeed
at all in time**. […] Therefore it would be correctly said
that the world was not created in time, but that time
had its existence in consequence of the world. For it
is the motion of the heaven that has displayed the
nature of time (Philo, *Allegorical Interpretation*, II - Part
2, emphasis mine).

For Philo, *six days* is not what one is to understand from the
Genesis account but rather, the number *six* and all of its amazing
mathematical properties is what is to be appreciated. His concept of time is that it is in itself a created thing. On that point
most scientists would agree, evolutionists and creationists alike,
that time was created along with space and that space and time

cannot be separated.[38] Because Philo does not see time beginning until the creation of the sun, what can we conclude regarding how long the first four days were? Obviously, if they came into being outside of time, as he suggests, then it is impossible to discuss their duration since that would be an oxymoron by definition. Consequently, the assertion that Philo in any way held to the belief in a universe that was billions of years old, as the Progressive Creation position suggests, is simply unfounded. Conversely, we see from Philo's paraphrase of Genesis 1 (in which he stated that according to Moses the world was created in six literal days) what he thinks the deeper meaning of six days actually is:

> When, therefore, Moses says, "God completed his works on the sixth day," we must understand that he is speaking not of **a number of days**, but that he **takes six as a perfect number**. Since it is the first number which is equal in its parts, in the half, and the third and sixth parts, and since it is produced by the multiplication of two unequal factors, two and three (Philo *Allegorical Interpretation*, II - Part 3, emphasis mine).

Philo and the Number Six

Philo is not arguing about how long a day was. He was not saying that they were long indefinite ages in which God did His handiwork. In no way is his statement grounds for proving that he, as an ancient interpreter, believed that those days were indefinite and therefore allowed for enough time for evolution to occur. Rather he was saying that it wasn't six *days*, but really just about the number six which he continues to describe as a "perfect number." For Philo, the argument isn't about the days, but about the incredible features of the number of six. Philo has not even considered how long the days were, but thought that a deeper truth to be mined from the Scriptures was the profoundness of the mathematical qualities of *six* as a number.

We may not be able to pin Philo down on exactly how long he thought the creation took. If we simply accept at face value what he said in the beginning of his treatise, then we could just conclude that according to Moses, God took six literal days though looking at his allegory, we see a different picture. However, it can hardly be denied that his consideration of the six days has nothing to do with time but everything to do with the number six as a mathematical entity worthy of contemplation. Thus, we leave Philo fairly convinced that on the literal plain, he believed that Genesis 1 did indeed refer to the creation of heaven and earth in six literal, 24-hour days and from an allegorical point of view believed the *six* to be included because it was a perfect number.

7-"Days" According to the Church Fathers

> We assert that Moses spoke in the literal sense, not allegorically or figuratively, i.e., that the world, with all its creatures, was created within six days, as the words read (Martin Luther, *Lectures on Genesis*).

The Early Church Fathers

The early Church Fathers were men who believed in Jesus as their Savior and Lord and were the leaders of the church after the time of the original twelve apostles. They defended and proclaimed the death and resurrection of Jesus and the Bible as a whole. Their writings show us that they spent great amounts of time attempting to disprove false teachings that arose. The issue of creation was certainly one of those.

The Church Fathers wrote against the Greek teaching that there was not a beginning, that the universe was infinite. They also wrote against spontaneous generation, which taught that life merely sprang up all by itself without a Creator—which has similarities to the ideas of Charles Darwin known today as abiogenesis. We need to keep in mind, as stated earlier, that just because the Church Fathers have a particular interpretation of a passage, it does not automatically mean that we have to agree with them. They were men who could make mistakes and their writings are not considered inspired like the Bible. However, they are indicative of what the early church believed Scripture was teaching. Because of the sheer number of their writings, we will only look at the most salient of writers; just the ante-Nicene Fathers (the writings of the Fathers from approximately the second until the fourth century AD) who wrote thousands of pages—enough to occupy a lifetime of study.

Twisting the Words of the Early Fathers

The Church Fathers, like the ancient Jewish writers, have been appealed to by those who believe in an old earth to establish that the Bible truly teaches that the heavens and earth are very old. As we noted earlier, Dr. Ross has claimed that many of the Church Fathers believed in an old earth rather than in a young earth.

It is twisting the facts, however, to say that "many of the early Church Fathers [...] interpret the creation days [...] as long periods of time" (Ross 1991: 141). We have already demonstrated that Josephus, whom he includes in his list, thought just the opposite and dates the age of the world to about 5,800 years. In a similar fashion, the vast majority of early Church Fathers believed that Genesis 1–2 spoke of literal days, not long periods of time.

Ross's poor scholarship has unfortunately led many to believe that the Church Fathers believed in day-ages when in fact they did not. Dr. Joshua Zorn discusses how he used to believe in a young earth and was very zealous until he learned more about science and in particular, read that the ancient Jewish and Christian interpreters believed in long days of creation.

> For me it was surprising to find out that very few of the early Jewish interpreters or Church Fathers held to the six consecutive twenty-four-hour day interpretation of Genesis 1. In *Creation and Time*, Ross has documented that Philo, Justin Martyr, Irenaeus, Hippolytus,

Clement of Alexandra, Origin, Augustine, Basil, and others all held to other interpretations (Zorn 1997: 3).

Contrary to what Hugh Ross claims, practically none of the Church Fathers believed in long days of creation, which explains Zorn's surprise. Again, we note that the Church Fathers are not the standard by which we measure Scripture; they were fallible. They do, however, provide a window into how ancient believers understood and interpreted Scripture. If nearly every ancient interpreter understood the days of Genesis to be literal, then there exists no historical basis to believe in anything but six literal days of creation.

Let's survey what some of the Church Fathers thought about Genesis 1 and 2 and whether they indeed support the position that the universe and the earth are billions of years old.

Barnabas

The Epistle of Barnabas[39] was probably written between 70 AD and 135 AD possibly by an Alexandrian Jew, though authorship is not clear. "The Epistle of Barnabas is, like I Clement, really anonymous ..." (Lake 1912: 337–339). While we are not so concerned with proving who indeed actually wrote it, we are interested in mining the interpretation of an ancient Christian regarding the creation. From chapter 15 on, covering the topic of the false and the true Sabbath, we read:

> Further, also, it is written concerning the Sabbath in the Decalogue which [the Lord] spoke, face to face, to Moses on Mount Sinai, "And sanctify ye the Sabbath of the Lord with clean hands and a pure heart"… The Sabbath is mentioned at **the beginning of the creation** [thus]: "And God made in six days the works of His hands, and made an end on the seventh day, and rested on it, and sanctified it." Attend, my children, to the meaning of this expression, **"He finished in six days."** This implieth that the Lord will finish all things

in six thousand years, for a day is with Him a thousand years (emphasis mine).

Contrary to believing in an old earth and universe, this author believed that the total span of earth's history would last seven thousand years and then God would "make a beginning of the eighth day, that is, a beginning of another world." How much more clarity in a creation time line could one ask for? This author was by far not the only one to hold to the belief that the six literal days of creation, multiplied by one thousand, was equal the total time in years which the earth would exist. It would also be wrong to conclude that the author somehow thought that the days in Genesis were not actual days. It is precisely because those days were real, literal days that the formula worked in his mind. Because the days of creation were real and definite units of time, so too would be the duration of earth's history—a grand total of seven thousand years.

Irenaeus

Irenaeus, an early church father of the second century in the area of modern-day France, in his work, *Against Heresies*, reiterates the formula the author of the Epistle of Barnabas so plainly put forth. Irenaeus says:

> **For in as many days as this world was made, in so many thousand years shall it be concluded.** And for this reason the Scripture says: "Thus the heaven and the earth were finished, and all their adornment. And God brought to a conclusion upon the sixth day the works that He had made; and God rested upon the seventh day from all His works" (Genesis 2:2). This is an account of the things formerly created, as also it is a prophecy of what is to come. For the day of the Lord is as a thousand years; (2 Peter 3:8) **and in six days created things were completed:** it is evident, therefore, that they will come to an end at the sixth thousand

year (Irenaeus *Against Heresies* Book 5 Chapter 28, emphasis mine).

Irenaeus is discussing the end of the age, but plainly believed the days of creation to be literal. "For in as many days as this world was made, in so many thousand years shall it be concluded." Irenaeus believed that the world would end after six thousand years precisely because the creation was finished after six days. If we reverse the formula where one day equals one thousand years, then there is no other conclusion that may be drawn concerning how long he believed those first days of creation to be. If God will rest after six thousand years, and if the formula is that one thousand years equals a day, then the days of creation must be nothing other than 24-hour days. If the number of years until the end of the world is believed to be definite and concrete by Irenaeus, then he must have believed that the days of creation were literal as well.

Theophilus of Antioch

Theophilus of Antioch, born around 115 AD and died about 185 AD, was a prolific writer of the early church. Theophilus was an apologist especially concerned with refuting the false teachers of his day. Theophilus, writing to "Autolycus an Idolater and Scorner of Christians," states concerning the six days of creation that,

> Of this six days' work no man can give a worthy explanation and description of all its parts ... on account of the exceeding greatness and riches of the wisdom of God which there is in the six days' work above narrated (Theophilus: Book 1, Chapter 1).

He later says, "But the power of God is shown in this, that, first of all, He creates out of nothing, according to His will, the things that are made" (Chapter 8). He thus establishes that, contrary to Greek thought, there was nothing before God began His work of creation. Interestingly, in light of the evolution plus

God theories, Theophilus writes concerning the creation of the luminaries and how God created them later so as to confound the vain philosophers.

> On the fourth day the luminaries were made; because God, Who possesses foreknowledge, knew the follies of the vain philosophers, that they were going to say, that **the things which grow on the earth are produced** from the heavenly bodies, so as to exclude God. In order, therefore, that the truth might be obvious, the plants and seeds were produced prior to the heavenly bodies, for what is posterior cannot produce that which is prior (Book 2, Chapter 15, emphasis mine).

God Finished in Six Days

The current evolutionary (abiogenesis) model teaches that life spontaneously generated in the primordial soup of the earth. A necessary condition for the generation of life was the presence of the sun to provide the light, warmth, and energy for that life to miraculously begin. Theophilus, who obviously knew nothing of the paradigm of biological evolution, seems to have pre-empted the idea. The thought of spontaneous generation did not begin with Darwin; it was a belief held by the ancient Greeks. Theophilus was specifically attacking the belief that the sun was necessary for the generation of plant life. It is also significant that those holding both evolutionary timescale and the Bible as being true (Progressive Creation and Theistic Evolution) have to reinterpret the text of Genesis 1 to make it fit their preconceptions. Theophilus, however, wrote extensively to disprove such theories that contradicted the Scriptures as he understood them. He then gives a summary statement of all that God had done, "God, having thus completed the heavens, the earth, the sea, and all that are in them, on the sixth day, rested on the seventh day from all His works which He made" (Chapter XIX). Later in chapter 23 he states again:

> Man, therefore, God made on the sixth day, and made known this creation after the seventh day, when also

He made Paradise, that he might be in a better and distinctly superior place. And that this is true, the fact itself proves. For how can one miss seeing that the pains which women suffer in childbed, and the oblivion of their labours which they afterwards enjoy, are sent in order that the word of God may be fulfilled, and that the race of men may increase and multiply? And do we not see also the judgment of the serpent,—how hatefully he crawls on his belly and eats the dust,—that we may have this, too, for a proof of the things which were said aforetime? (Book 2, Chapter 23).

According to his logic, the facts that we see the pains associated with childbirth and that snakes do indeed crawl on their bellies proves that God created just as Genesis declared. Whether or not we agree with his logic is irrelevant. What is important for our study is to see that another church father understood the events of Genesis 1–3 as very real and literal events. They were historical events. The days were literal days. To further confirm those facts, Theophilus establishes that the fall of man and the deception of the woman were at the beginning. This makes perfect sense if the days of creation were only six, real days, but not if creation lasted billions of years as Theistic Evolution and Progressive Creationism purport. "This Eve, on account of her having been in the **beginning** deceived by the serpent [...]" (Chapter 28, emphasis mine).

Theophilus' Simple Arithmetic

Many old earth advocates suggest that belief in a young earth of about six thousand years is a fairly recent one. Theophilus apparently wasn't aware that he was supposed to believe in an old earth as we have already demonstrated. But just to let us know what he really thought, he left us yet another clear proof that he thought that creation had taken place only several thousand years before his own time. In book 3, chapter 23, he endeavored to demonstrate that the prophets of the Old Testament were more ancient than the Greek writers. He states:

> And that we may give a more accurate exhibition of
> **eras and dates**, we will, God helping us, now give an
> account not only of the dates after the deluge, but also
> of those before it, so as to reckon the **whole number
> of all the years**, as far as possible; **tracing up to the
> very beginning of the creation of the world**, which
> Moses the servant of God recorded through the Holy
> Spirit. For having first spoken of what concerned the
> creation and genesis of the world, and of the first man,
> and all that happened after in the order of events, he
> signified also the years that elapsed before the deluge
> (emphasis mine).

Theophilus immediately begins chapter 24 with a very literal totaling of the years of Adam and his descendants and arrives at a number fairly close to what young earth advocates propose:

> Adam lived till he begat a son, 230 years. And his
> son Seth, 205 [...] And his son Enoch, 165 [...] And
> Lamech's son was Noah, of whom we have spoken
> above, who begat Shem when 500 years old. During
> Noah's life, in his 600th year, the flood came. **The total
> number of years, therefore, till the flood, was 2242**
> (emphasis mine).

Theophilus has done nothing extraordinary here. He has merely added up the lifetimes from Adam until Noah and arrived at a number of years of 2,242; that is Adam was created 2,242 years before the flood (an event which he considered literal and real). He then continues:

> And immediately after the flood, Shem, who was 100
> years old, begat Arphaxad. [...] And his son Eber, when
> 134. And from him the Hebrews name their race [...]
> And his son Nahor, when 75. And his son Terah, when
> 70. And his son Abraham, our patriarch, begat Isaac
> when he was 100 years old. **Until Abraham, therefore,
> there are 3278 years** (emphasis mine).

Thus from the creation (including Adam) to Abraham, according to Theophilus, there were 3,278 years. Therefore, if we add up Theophilus' calculations until the present we get: Adam to Abraham 3,278 years (Abraham lived somewhere about 2000 BC) plus 2,000 years approximately from Abraham until Christ and then another 2,000 from Christ until the present to equal 7,278 years from the beginning until now. Where is the belief in long, indefinite ages in the distant past that Theophilus was supposed to believe in? Theophilus reiterates his point (and I submit here, at the risk of being redundant, merely to stress that this writer is not being taken out of context, nor am I leaving out important elements of his treatise) because he fully desired to prove as clearly as possible that the world was only thousands of years old:

> And from the foundation of the world the whole time is thus traced, so far as its main epochs are concerned. From the creation of the world to the deluge were 2242 years. And from the deluge to the time when Abraham our forefather begat a son, 1036 years. And from Isaac, Abraham's son, to the time when the people dwelt with Moses in the desert, 660 years. And from the death of Moses and the rule of Joshua the son of Nun, to the death of the patriarch David, 498 years. And from the death of David and the reign of Solomon to the sojourning of the people in the land of Babylon, 518 years 6 months 10 days. And from the government of Cyrus to the death of the Emperor Aurelius Verus, 744 years. **All the years from the creation of the world amount to a total of 5698 years, and the odd months and days** (Book 3, Chapter 28, emphasis mine).

To Theophilus, the Earth Is Young

For fear that his reader might get lost in all of these numbers and hence forget the reason for their listing, he plainly states that he is writing to show as nonsense the positions of the writers that suggest that the world is extremely old:

> For my purpose is not to furnish mere matter of much talk, but to throw light upon **the number of years from the foundation of the world**, and to condemn the empty labour and trifling of these authors, **because there have neither been twenty thousand times ten thousand years** [200,000,000] from the flood to the present time, as Plato said, affirming that there had been so many years; nor yet 15 times 10,375 years [155,625], as we have already mentioned Apollonius the Egyptian gave out; nor is the world uncreated, **nor is there a spontaneous production of all things** [abiogensis], as Pythagoras and the rest dreamed; but, being indeed created, it is also governed by the providence of God, who made all things; and the whole course of time and the years are made plain to those who wish to obey the truth (Book 3, Chapter 26, emphasis mine).

For Theophilus, believing that the world is two hundred million years old is complete nonsense invented by those who are not seeking the truth. He is humble enough to concede that his calculations might be off by a little bit.

> For if even a chronological error has been committed by us, of, e.g., 50 or 100, or even 200 years, yet not of thousands and tens of thousands, as Plato and Apollonius and other mendacious authors have hitherto written (Chapter 29).

He is not dogmatic about his calculation being the only correct number. However, he is suggesting that to speculate that the earth is over one hundred thousand years old as Plato suggests or is two hundred million years is complete nonsense. Theophilus wrote to "condemn the empty labour and trifling of these authors." While his opinion doesn't prove that Genesis teaches a young earth, it does prove that a young earth was considered orthodox and the only acceptable, biblical perspective. In light of all the other ancient commentators hereto examined, we are gaining a picture that to believe in an old earth of hundreds of thousands, or millions, let alone billions of years would have been considered extremely aberrant and outrageous.

Clement of Alexandria

Clement of Alexandria, who lived from 153 to 217 AD, is considered one of the most influential of the early Church Fathers. He was a prolific writer who so eloquently articulated many matters of faith in his generation. He wrote briefly but succinctly concerning the time frame of the creation:

> For the creation of the world was concluded in six days. For the motion of the sun from solstice to solstice is completed in six months—in the course of which, at one time the leaves fall, and at another plants bud and seeds come to maturity. And they say that the embryo is perfected exactly in the sixth month, that is, in one hundred and eighty days in addition to the two and a half, as Polybus the physician relates in his book *On the Eighth Month*, and Aristotle the philosopher in his book *On Nature*. Hence the Pythagoreans, as I think, reckon six the perfect number, from the creation of the world (*The Stromata* Book 6, Chapter 16).

We know that he believed in a literal six days by the examples that he gives (e.g., the motion of the sun, the time the leaves fall, the budding of plants, and the time of perfecting of an embryo at six months). From the fact that his examples, which all have to do with a unit of six, are nonetheless real and finite units of time, we can conclude that his understanding of the first days of time were no different.

Hippolytus

Hippolytus was a bishop of Rome who lived from 170 to 236 AD and was a student of Irenaeus. In his book, *The Refutation of All*

Heresies (book 4, chapter 48), he says, "For in six days the world was made, and (the Creator) rested on the seventh." What does he mean by six days, though? Could it be that he is referring to six ages—ages in which millions and billions of years might have elapsed? How can we know precisely what he meant by six days?

Fortunately, Hippolytus continues in a very direct and exact manner. He would not have his ancient audience, or us for that matter, be in the dark regarding what he firmly believed the Scriptures to be teaching:

> But that we may not leave our subject at this point undemonstrated, we are obliged to discuss the matter of the times, of which a man should not speak hastily, because they are a light to him. For as the times are noted from the foundation of the world, and reckoned from Adam, they set clearly before us the matter with which our inquiry deals. For the first appearance of our Lord in the flesh took place in Bethlehem, under Augustus, in the year 5500; and He suffered in the thirty-third year. And 6,000 years must needs be accomplished, in order that the Sabbath may come, the rest, the holy day "on which God rested from all His works" (*The Extant Works and Fragments of Hippolytus,* Part 1.3.4).

Here he unambiguously declares the earth to be young. According to his calculations, Jesus came in the flesh 5,500 years after the foundation of the world. He then states that the entirety of human history would last only six thousand years, a theme that we have seen several times earlier in our study of the other ancient commentators.[40] There exists no doubt in the mind of Hippolytus that God created all that there is a mere 5,500 years before Jesus and that the entire span of history would last no longer than six thousand years.

Origen and Methodius

At this point we need to consider Origen and Methodius, both of whom were on Hugh Ross's list of Church Fathers who supposedly believed in non-literal days of creation and hence an old earth. We need to consider them in tandem since they are better understood together rather than separately regarding creation. Origen lived in Alexandria from 185 to 254 AD. He was a follower of Jesus Christ, who, unfortunately, began interpreting the Scriptures in a manner that was considered heretical by the Christian community of his day and for centuries after.

Origen's Disturbing Doctrines

Of all the Church Fathers that we have examined so far, Origen is the only one that truly did reject the literal interpretation of the text of Genesis in favor of an allegorical approach in order to resolve some of the seeming difficulties of the text. While Origen's love for God is not in question, his method of interpretation is. For in caring more about the hidden meaning of the text than the literal and plain meaning, mixed with the NeoPlatonistic thinking of Alexandria, Origen wrote some very disturbing things concerning doctrines which are essential to orthodox Christianity; and if one merely follows the plain meaning of Scripture, these cannot be missed. Though Origen was perhaps the first to systematize a doctrine of the Trinity, his conclusions are not derived from the plain reading of Scripture, but from mixing Greek philosophy, allegory, and Scripture together. Below is an excerpt from Origen on the Trinity:

> The God and Father, who holds the universe together, is superior to every being that exists, for he imparts to each one from his own existence that which each one is; the Son, being less than the Father, is superior to rational creatures alone (for he is second to the Father); the Holy Spirit is still less, and dwells within the saints alone. So that in this way the power of the Father is greater than that of the Son and of the Holy Spirit, and

that of the Son is more than that of the Holy Spirit, and in turn the power of the Holy Spirit exceeds that of every other holy being (Moore 2006).

Origen obviously holds to a completely unorthodox position of the relation of the three persons of the Trinity to such an extent that it sounds much like the modern-day cult of Jehovah's Witnesses who hold that Jesus is the first of all of God's creations but is not equal to God. Obviously someone holding to such a position is unstable in their interpretation of the Bible and should not be looked to for guidance on interpreting the creation account of Genesis. We might be tempted to give Origen the benefit of the doubt concerning his heretical view of the Trinity. However, it is not only this issue but many others that call into question his teachings.

Another example which is nowhere to be found in the pages of Scripture, but purely from his own imagination, is the creation of souls. This teaching held that not only were there many beings created prior to the act of creation which originally fell away from their Creator, but that the soul of Christ was among that number.

Where do we see this idea even remotely intimated in Scripture? Obviously, the answer is absolutely nowhere! Isn't the plain teaching of Scripture easy for all to see? Jesus said, "before Abraham was, I am" (John 8:58) and the Jews obviously understood what He was saying since they wanted to stone Him! In Revelation 1:17 Jesus said that He is the first and the last—a term that is used only for God and stands in direct contradiction to Origen's teaching.

Methodius Opposed to Origen's Teaching

We now turn our attention to Methodius who was born shortly after Origen and became bishop over Olympus and Patara in Lycia and then later died as a martyr around 312 AD in Greece. He was chiefly known as an ardent opponent of the teachings of Origen and devoted numerous pages to refuting his heretical teachings. In a fragment of his writings[41], he says concerning Origen, whom he then quotes:

> Origen, after having fabled many things concerning the eternity of the universe, adds this also:
>
> > Nor yet from Adam, as some say, did man, previously not existing, first take his existence and come into the world. Nor again did the world begin to be made six days before the creation of Adam. But if any one should prefer to differ in these points, let him first say, whether a period of time be not easily reckoned from the creation of the world, according to the Book of Moses, to those who so receive it, the voice of prophecy here proclaiming: "Thou art God from everlasting, and world without end [...] For a thousand years in Thy sight are but as yesterday: seeing that is past as a watch in the night" (Psalm 90:2, Psalm 90:4). For when a thousand years are reckoned as one day in the sight of God, and from the creation of the world to His rest is six days, so also to our time, six days are defined, as those say who are clever arithmeticians. Therefore, they say that an age of six thousand years extends from Adam to our time. For they say that the judgment will come on the seventh day, that is in the seventh thousand years. Therefore, all the days from our time to that which was in the beginning, in which God created the heaven and the earth, are computed to be thirteen days; before which God, because he had as yet created nothing according to their folly, is stripped of His name of Father and Almighty. But if there are thirteen days in the sight of God from the creation of the world, how can Wisdom say, in the Book of the Son of Sirach: "Who can number the sand of the sea, and the drops of rain, and the days of eternity?" (Ecclus. 1:2).

> **This is what Origen says seriously, and mark how
> he trifles** (Methodius *Extracts from the Work on Things
> Created*, emphasis mine).

The last line of the above quote contains the final remarks of
Methodius. Notice that where Origen denied the literal creation
in six days, Methodius just dismisses his words as "trifles." Thus,
we can truly admit that there was at least one who thought that
the creation of the heavens and earth exceeded six literal days.
However, the idea is considered to be foolish and is rejected out
of hand and Origen is the only known exception to the rule. It
must also be kept in mind that Origen's denial of such teachings
of the creation was a result of his allegorical and NeoPlatonistic
method of interpreting the Scriptures—the same method that led
him to teach that the Holy Spirit is inferior in essence to the Son
and the Son is inferior in essence to the Father. He thought, in
fact, both the Son and the Holy Spirit were created beings. This
same method also led him to teach the preexistence of souls and
the soul of Christ—a doctrine that resounds with the teachings
of the Mormon cult started by Joseph Smith.

Fathers of the
Third and Fourth Centuries

In 312 AD Constantine the Great conquered the city of Rome,
the center of the oppressive government which for nearly three
centuries had afflicted Christians with all manners of torture and
martyrdom.

> A vision had assured him that he should conquer in
> the sign of the Christ, and his warriors carried **Christ's
> monogram** on their shields, though the majority of
> them were pagans ... Of his gratitude to the **God** of
> the **Christians** the victor immediately gave convincing
> proof; the **Christian worship** was henceforth tolerated
> throughout the empire (Edict of Milan, early in 313)
> (Catholic Encyclopedia 2006, emphasis mine).

Constantine's victory marked the beginning of a new age for the church where almost overnight the belief in Jesus as Lord went from being threatened with a miserable death to being accepted as the official state religion.

Victorinus

Victorinus, a church father who flourished around 270 AD and was martyred around 303 AD, wrote many works, most having been lost, unfortunately. Nevertheless, one that was preserved titled "On the Creation of the World" contains some candid reflections upon what he understood those six days to mean.

> To me, as I meditate and consider in my mind concerning the creation of this world in which we are kept enclosed, even such is the rapidity of that creation; as is contained in the book of Moses, which he wrote about its creation, and which is called Genesis. God produced that entire mass for the adornment of His majesty in six days; on the seventh to which He consecrated it […] **In the beginning God made the light, and divided it in the exact measure of twelve hours by day and by night, for this reason** […] (Victorinus, emphasis mine).

Note that Victorinus specifically states that God created in a matter of six days and rested on the seventh. He then further defines for us what he means by a day by saying that God divided the day and the night into 12-hour segments and hence a 24-hour day. Could we ask for a more specific explanation from an ancient source as to what they understood a day to be?

Victorinus is hardly alone in his understanding of the creation days consisting of 24 hours. Basil "The Great" (ca. 330 to 379 AD) corroborates Victorinus' teaching one hundred years later with his statement:

> 'And there was evening and morning, one day.' Why did he say 'one' and not 'first'? **He said 'one' because**

> he was defining the measure of day and night [...]
> since twenty-four hours fill up the interval of one
> day (*The Six Days Work* 1:1–2, emphasis mine).

Lactantius

Lactantius (260 to 330 AD), who suffered under the last of the persecutions of Rome, in his latter years had the unique fortune of being the tutor of Constantine's son Crispus. Working in such close proximity to the emperor, he was given the opportunity to become "the instrument of Providence in bearing the testimony of Jesus, 'even before kings'" (*Fathers* Volume 7 Introduction Lactantius). Lactantius thus becomes an important voice concerning our question of how the Church Fathers interpreted Genesis. His perspective is especially noteworthy since he had tasted the bitterness of suffering for Christ and then later witnessed the introduction of Christianity as the official state religion, which ultimately led to his working in the home of the emperor himself. We can surmise, therefore, that he would have desired to be bold in his declaration of Christ and to teach the Scriptures as faithfully as possible.

In his work *The Divine Institutes*, which he entitled, "Of the First and Last Times of the World," he states that God made the heavens and earth in six days. He also straightforwardly states:

> Plato and many others of the philosophers, since they were ignorant of the origin of all things, and of that primal period at which the world was made, **said that many thousands of ages had passed** since this beautiful arrangement of the world was completed; foolishly say that they possess comprised in their memorials **four hundred and seventy thousand years**; in which matter [...] they believed that they were at liberty to speak falsely. But we, whom the Holy Scriptures instruct to the knowledge of the truth, know the beginning and the end of the world [...] **Therefore let the philosophers, who enumerate thousands of ages from the beginning of the world, know that the**

six thousandth year is not yet completed, and that when this number is completed the consummation must take place, and the condition of human affairs be remodeled for the better, the proof of which must first be related, that the matter itself may be plain. **God completed the world and this admirable work of nature in the space of six days,** as is contained in the secrets of Holy Scripture, and consecrated the seventh day, on which He had rested from His works (*The Divine Institutes*, Chapter 16, emphasis mine).

Lactantius states this as clearly and plainly as one could possibly expect. He unambiguously declares that it is the philosophers who are both ignorant and foolish in declaring that the origin of all things took place over hundreds of thousands of years earlier. Lactantius even denounces an exact amount of 475,000 years and if it was considered foolish to think that the world was so old in his day, why should we be persuaded that the earth is 4.56 billion years old and the universe is about 14 billion years old? We have seen again and again that the ancient interpreters believed that Scripture taught a young earth.

Augustine

Of all the Church Fathers (besides Origen), the person we would expect to hold to a view of an old earth and a creation week that took place over vast ages would be Augustine. He lived from 354 to 430 AD and was the bishop of Hippo in North Africa. He is considered to be the foremost theologian of the Catholic Church and is also held in high esteem by many Protestants. A typical method of interpretation for him was allegorical and typological. He often sought a *deeper* and spiritual truth underlying a given text. Thus, to discover that he did not believe that the creation week happened over long periods of time, as Dr. Ross has stated, is surprising. Ironically, Augustine held to a view that God created everything in an instant rather than in six literal days. However, as to when this occurred, he, like so many Church Fathers before him, believed the creation to have occurred less than six thousand years before his own time.

Creation Was Less than Six Thousand Years Ago

In his monumental work, *City of God* book 12, chapter 10, Augustine lucidly comments on certain people that just don't have their facts straight concerning the age of the earth:

> They are deceived, too, by those highly mendacious documents which profess to give the history of many thousand years, though, reckoning by the sacred writings, **we find that not 6,000 years have yet passed** (*City of God* book 12, chapter 10, emphasis mine).

He then reiterates this in chapter 12.

> As to those who are always asking why man was not created during these countless ages of the infinitely extended past, and came into being so lately that, **according to Scripture, less than 6,000 years have elapsed since He began to be,** I would reply to them regarding the creation of man, just as I replied regarding the origin of the world to those who will not believe that it is not eternal, but had a beginning, which even Plato himself most plainly declares [...] **If it offends them that the time that has elapsed since the creation of man is so short, and his years so few according to our authorities** [...] (*City of God* book 12, chapter 12, emphasis mine).

Even Augustine, the one person in addition to Origen that we might have expected to see an earth of billions of years or hundreds of thousands at the very least, held to a young earth. One, therefore, cannot argue that he was advocating any type of day-age theory. Nor did he envision any gap between the verses 1, 2, or 3. However, we may not conclude that he believed in a literal six-day creation either.

Augustine's "Literal" Interpretation

Augustine's denial of six actual days is trumpeted by Davis Young, of the geology department of Calvin College Grand Rapids, Michigan, who notes that Augustine's "literal" interpretation of Genesis does not resemble the modern literal six days creation week or young earth positions.

> He [Augustine] later came to reject that [allegorical] method and in this more mature work, written in his late fifties just before *The City of God*, he is concerned 'to discuss Sacred Scriptures according to the plain meaning of the historical facts, not according to future events which they foreshadow'. **Given his strong commitment to literal interpretation, it is fascinating to recognize that the outcome bears absolutely no resemblance to modern literal interpretations.** For example, **he concludes that in Genesis I the terms "light," "day," and "morning" bear a spiritual, rather than physical, meaning.** Yet for Augustine, spiritual light is just as literal as physical light, and the creation of spiritual light is just as much a historical event or fact as the creation of physical light. **What is literal for one person may not be literal for others** (Young 1988, emphasis mine).

According to Young, Augustine stresses that his new work is literal and not metaphorical or allegorical. He then goes on to state that since Augustine was such a great theologian we ought to listen to his testimony. Young writes,

> From his general approach to this text, it would appear that Augustine, the great theologian, a man saturated in Holy Scripture, actually **encourages the church not to cling dogmatically to specific renderings of the text but to rethink its interpretations in the light of genuine extra-biblical knowledge.** Perhaps we should pay him serious attention. Augustine is obviously interested in the science of his own day and interacts

with it. He takes extra-biblical knowledge seriously (Young 1988, emphasis mine).

Notice that Young urges us to follow Augustine's example to shift our interpretation of Genesis "in the light of genuine extra-biblical knowledge." It would seem that Young is suggesting that we are to allow modern humanistic thought to act as a standard by which we interpret Scripture. Consider that he says, "Augustine shows respect for scientific activity, and does not want to put Scripture in a situation of conflict with it" (Young 1988). Certainly Young is correct that none of us ought to disregard scientific activity nor pit the Bible against *science*. However, when the scientific activity of which he speaks contradicts the historical-grammatical reading of the Bible, then there will be conflict.

Spontaneous Generation a Fact for Augustine

It would seem that Young is so eager to demonstrate that we should emulate Augustine by not holding to the belief that God created the heavens and earth in six (real, literal) days that he advocates believing man's shifting thoughts over the Bible. Consider how his next statement and following example encourage believing in (faulty and secular) science rather than merely trusting the Bible, even when it disagrees with man's findings.

> For example, it is clear that he [Augustine] accepts spontaneous generation of organisms and the four elements of Greek thought. He expends considerable effort in relating Genesis I to the four elements and to the Greek theory of natural places: "One must surely not think that in this passage of Holy Scripture there has been an omission of any one of the four elements that are generally supposed to make up the world just because there seems to be no mention of air in the account of sky, water, and earth" (Young 1988).

Are we therefore to allow mainstream thought about the origins of the universe, which, as we have seen, is built on a paradigm that all matter and all life arose by chance, merely because

Augustine held a belief that was sympathetic to the science of his day? Exactly what point Young wished to make regarding Augustine's belief in spontaneous generation is unclear. There exist two possibilities as I see it: either Young believes that that confirms the teaching of evolution and its teaching of abiogenesis or that just as Augustine permitted current thought to influence his interpretation of Scripture, so too should we. In either case, our response is a resounding "no" since neither could be further from what our response should be.

If Young meant to demonstrate that Augustine was in fact rather progressive for his day to believe in spontaneous generation, then it only serves to prove why Scripture alone should be our standard. Wikipedia, the grass-roots, online encyclopedia intended to just give popular entries, rightly describes the history of spontaneous generation:

> Classical notions of abiogenesis, now more precisely known as **spontaneous generation**, held that complex, living organisms are generated by decaying organic substances, e.g. that mice spontaneously appear in stored grain or maggots spontaneously appear in meat.
>
> Yet it was not until 1862 that Louis Pasteur performed a series of careful experiments which conclusively proved that a truly sterile medium would remain sterile.
>
> Three years earlier, *Darwin's On the Origin of Species by Means of Natural Selection* (published in 1859), had presented an argument that modern organisms had evolved, over immense periods of time, from simpler ancestral forms, that species changed over time. Darwin himself declined to speculate on some implications of his theory—that at some point there may have existed an un-organism with no prior ancestor and that such an organism may have come into existence, formed from non-living molecules.

> Pasteur had demonstrated that spontaneous genera-
> tion was wrong, and he also seemed to have demon-
> strated that any concept involving the generation of
> living matter from non-living matter was also wrong
> (Wikipedia.com: *Abiogenesis*, emphasis mine).

Spontaneous generation is a theory that has been scientifically proven to be false and worthless. Thus to assert that it was in any way good that Augustine paid heed to the scientific activity of his day rather than merely believe the, albeit unpopular, teaching of the Bible, is not only fallacious but inexcusable. It is unfortunate that Augustine held to such a position that has now without a doubt been proven bogus and incorrect. Augustine's endorsement of "the four elements" does not need to even be mentioned.

I would argue that rather than trying to absorb Augustine's views, we hold fast to the easy teaching of Scripture and where Augustine or anyone for that matter agrees with it, then we embrace their views and when they differ we part ways. Augustine was wrong about interpreting Scripture in light of what Young described as "genuine extra-biblical knowledge." Spontaneous generation and only four elements were the prevailing thought back then. Using them to interpret the Bible led to false conclusions in his day and interpreting the Bible through the lens of evolutionary thought today will lead to faulty conclusions about God and the world in our day.

Augustine certainly made important contributions to the church and those should not be discounted. However, the real and lasting contributions were those that were firmly based on Scripture and not on the changing *science* of men. Thus, we ought to learn from Augustine as Young suggested; we should learn from his mistake of trying to appeal to current scientific thought where it disagrees with the Bible. Sooner or later man's science will change but the Bible remains.

The Fathers
Believed in a Young Earth

Having looked at the classic ancient interpreters of the Bible, both Jewish and Christian, we can now ask ourselves what the ancient perspective was. Did they actually believe in an old earth as some purport or did they hold to a literal point of view? As we have seen in every instance (except for Origen and partly Augustine), both Jewish and Christian perspectives held that the heavens and the earth were created in six literal days and many of the commentators defined what a day is by stating that it meant 24 hours. Not one of them (except Origen) even remotely intimated that those six days of creation should be understood as long ages or that *day* meant anything other than a period of 24 hours. Time and again, they believed that God made all that is in a span of six, 24-hour days and they all thought that it occurred less than six thousand years before their own lives. Even Augustine wrote that the creation had occurred less than six thousand years before his own day. The real exception to the overwhelming and prevailing belief that God created in a span of six days less than six thousand years earlier was Origen and as we saw, so many of his teachings were considered heretical that his opinion on the creation of the world bears little weight. This view of a literal, six-day creation would remain as the only acceptable belief until the enlightenment and the advent of the geology of Charles Lyell and Darwin's evolutionary hypothesis.

Thomas Aquinas of the thirteenth century, considered to be one of the foremost theologians of the Catholic Church, stated: "'God called the light day' (since the word 'day' is also used to denote a space of 24 hours). Other instances of a similar use occur, as pointed out by Rabbi Moses" (Thomas Aquinas, *The Summa Theologica*).

Martin Luther, the great Protestant reformer of the sixteenth century, believed in a young earth as well.

> We know from Moses that the world was not in existence before 6,000 years ago [...] He [Moses] calls 'a spade a spade,' i.e., he employs the terms 'day' and 'evening' without allegory, just as we customarily do [...] we assert that Moses spoke in the literal sense, not allegorically or figuratively, i.e., that the world, with all its creatures, was created within six days, as the words read. If we do not comprehend the reason for this, let us remain pupils and leave the job of teacher to the Holy Spirit (Martin Luther, *Lectures on Genesis*).

This view is shared by John Calvin, who also lived in the sixteenth century, that the earth is less than six thousand years old, which implies that the days of creation were literal six days of 24-hours. In speaking of those that reject some of his teachings, he strongly declares:

> A rebellious spirit will display itself no less insolently when it hears that there are three persons in the divine essence, than when it hears that God when he created man foresaw every thing that was to happen to him. Nor will they abstain from their jeers when told that little more than five thousand years have elapsed since the creation of the world (John Calvin).

Thus what shall we conclude? Is it safe to venture that the early church believed that God created the universe in six literal days roughly six thousand years prior to their time? There exists no historical reason to believe in any other conclusion. We have also seen that there exists no philological, semantic, or syntactical reason in the Bible. The Bible never suggests that the Genesis days should be considered longer. The only reason that exists to believe that those days were long periods of time is because one has accepted as established fact and truth the evolutionary model, and hence, feels the need to fit those billions of years into the Bible. The amazing irony, however, is that evolution was devised to try to explain how we got here *without* the aid of a Creator.

8-What Did Adam Know On His First Day?

Naming the Animals

One of the tasks Adam was given on the first day of his creation was to name the animals, an act that demonstrated his dominion over them as God had prescribed (Genesis 1:26, 28). Yet, therein lies a supposed problem that the day-age theory would presumably solve: if those days were not day-ages and death had not entered until Adam sinned, then why would Adam give names to animals that denote their carnivorous nature (such as *bird of prey*)? The proponents of Progressive Creationism have suggested that Adam was familiar with death, even before the creation of Eve, which would explain why he would give the animals names that fit their ferocious nature. Progressive Creationist Richard Deem explains:

> When Adam was first put into the garden, God said that he could eat from any tree except the tree of the knowledge of good and evil (Genesis 2:15–17). God threatened that Adam would "surely die" if he broke this command. This threat makes no sense unless Adam had already seen the death of animals. There is no recorded reply of Adam asking what death was. If he had never seen death this would have been an

obvious question. This is strong biblical evidence that Adam had already seen the death of animals even before Eve was created. In addition, Adam's choice of names for the animals indicated that he had seen them kill other animals. For example, the Hebrew name for lion is derived from the Hebrew root that means "in the sense of violence." In addition, Adam named some of the predatory birds using a Hebrew word with the meaning "bird of prey." In naming the eagle, Adam used the Hebrew word whose root means to lacerate. So, Scripture suggests that there was animal death before the fall of Adam and Eve (Deem 2006a).

Suggesting that Adam must have known what death was first-hand in order to understand God's directive is nothing more than speculation and not necessary since any child can understand the idea of death without having a family member die. To suggest that Adam knew what death was based on the names of the animals is not logical. Furthermore, Deem has assumed that Adam spoke Hebrew. While it is possible that Hebrew was the original language, there is no way to be sure that Adam and Eve didn't speak a completely different language. The above author is putting words into Adam's mouth that are not in the text. Because the Bible is God's Word, we want to be careful not to add or subtract from it, but just understand what is given.

Did Adam really include in the name *lion* the meaning of "in a sense of violence"? We agree that when we look up the Hebrew word אריה *aryeh* in the popular *Strong's Dictionary*, the definition does in fact say "in a sense of violence." But this does not in any way imply that Adam while in the Garden of Eden was thinking to himself, "Gee, what should I call this animal? Hmm, well, it has big teeth and I *have seen* it kill and eat other animals! I need to call it something that is characteristic of its violent nature. I know! I will call it *aryeh* (or in English *violence*)."

The reality is that *Strong's Dictionary* and other lexicons sometimes make an educated guess. When compiling a lexicon (dictionary) of ancient languages, the authors study the available writings and begin to formulate their ideas from there. There is no master copy of original meanings that they can consult. Some words are much easier than others due to their high frequency. The meaning of others, which are used only once in the entire Bible, known as *hapax legomenon*, must be deduced from the surrounding vocabulary. An example of such an occurrence is found in Isaiah:

> The wild beasts of the desert shall also meet with the jackals, and the wild goat shall bleat to its companion; also the night creature (לילית *lilit*) shall rest there, and find for herself a place of rest (Isaiah 34:14).

The term *night creature* is the Hebrew word *lilit* which occurs only here in the entire Bible. Even if it were to have been uttered by Adam, this would not tell us what it means. Thus, the translation *night creature* is only an educated guess on the part of the translator due to its similarity to the Hebrew word לילה *layla* meaning *night*.

Parallelisms

Another tool the translator can use to help clarify a text is *parallelisms*. Parallelisms are times when the biblical author followed the word in question with a synonym in close proximity. We see this style of parallelism often in the Proverbs where an idea is expressed by two (or more) different words. Consider the following example from Proverbs 2:10–11:

> When wisdom enters your heart,
> And knowledge is pleasant to your soul,
> Discretion will preserve you;
> Understanding will keep you.

There are several clues that would help us understand if one or two of these words were difficult since each verse is a pair of words meaning approximately the same thing:

- *wisdom — knowledge*
- *heart—soul*
- *discretion—understanding*
- *preserve—keep*

The words in this passage are fairly easy, but we can see how if we didn't know one, we could make an educated guess based on the context and meaning of the other. This is how many words are ascribed their meaning in the Bible—not from looking at a lexicon or dictionary, but from studying the context in which the word is used; so too with the word *lion*. The various authors of Hebrew lexicons such as Strong's, Brown Driver Briggs (BDB), and others do not know the original meaning of the word. However, they have observed the animal *lion* and how it is generally portrayed in Scripture as "in a sense of violence." But we must recognize that "in a sense of violence" is not the true meaning of the word *lion*, which is the translation of the Hebrew *aryeh*. The same is true of the birds of prey. Adam, didn't look at them and say to himself, "Hmm … I think that I will name you 'bird of prey' (Hebrew *ayit* עיט)." Again, modern scholars don't know what the etymology of עיט (*ayit*) is so they gave it a general term "bird of prey" for that is what it is. Let's consider an example in English that is similar.

Etymologies

When we say *God* we are referring to the Supreme Being who is the Sovereign of the universe. Looking in *Collins' English Dictionary* we see that the definition of *God* is "a supernatural being, who is worshipped as the controller of some part of the universe or some aspect of life in the world or is the personification of some force." But what is the origin of the word? We have seen the definition of the word, but where did it come from? Does the origin stem from *supreme being*, or *powerful one*? Is it related to the word *good*?

To answer these questions we must consult an etymological dictionary which gives a history of the origin of words. According to the online *Etymological Dictionary*, *god* (or *God*) in old English did mean *Supreme Being*. That, however, is not the end of the story. In Proto-Indo-European, the predecessor to English, it was spelled *ghut*, which meant *that which is invoked*. Although some trace it to an alternate Proto-Indo-European root *ghu-to meaning poured*, from the root *gheu meaning to pour, pour a libation*. The etymological dictionary also notes that it is not related to the word *good*. So, we see in a word we use every day that it had an origin that probably none of us knew before. We might have thought that it was related to *good* since God is good and if not that, then at least it came from *Supreme Being*.

However, the original meaning is neither *Supreme Being* nor *good* but is rather *that which is invoked* or *poured*. This is informative since it demonstrates that a definition and origin (etymology) are not necessarily the same. Thus to suggest that Adam was familiar with death before the fall and therefore called the lion *violent* and eagles and vultures *birds of prey* is anachronistic. We simply don't know what Adam meant by the names that he gave. All that we know is that in the Bible, the Hebrew words *aryeh—lion* and *ayit—birds of prey* are the meanings of those words as derived by scholars according to how the words are used, not according to their original meaning.

Replenish the Earth and the Gap Theory

In Genesis 1:28 we read "... and God said unto them, Be fruitful, and multiply, and replenish the earth, and subdue it" (KJV). The King James Version's use of the word *replenish* has been seen by Gap Theorists as proof that the earth is old, since supposedly Adam and Eve are commanded to *fill again*. In fact, the idea that God commanded Adam and Eve not merely *to fill the earth* but *to fill the earth again*, stems from the Gap Theory.[42] The proponents of the Gap Theory believe that the billions of years of the age of the heavens and earth, as touted by evolutionistic thinking, is found between Genesis 1:1 and 1:2. Thus, did God command Adam and Eve to fill the earth for the very first time or to fill the earth again? Did they actually understand that they were to fill the earth again because the world prior to their creation had been destroyed?

Replenish/*Malu*

It is true, that in today's English, when we say replenish we mean filling up something that is depleted, something that was once full and is now empty. However, just less than two hundred years ago, *Webster's Dictionary* (1828) defined the word as, "To fill; to stock with numbers or abundance." We can see that the word has changed from meaning *fill* to *fill again* today. Of course, the answer ultimately lies not in English but in Hebrew.

The Hebrew word מלאו (*malu*) does not mean to *refill*, but simply to *fill*. It in no way connotes or implies to fill again. It just means *fill*. God gave the same command *to fill* in Genesis 9:1 to Noah after the flood as He did to Adam and Eve. There is no question that Noah was to fill the earth *again*, but that is not intrinsically implied by the word; God simply said to fill the earth. Likewise, to suggest that God commanded Adam and Eve to repopulate a world that had been recreated is poor exegesis and is not even remotely supported from the text. We can, therefore, absolutely conclude that Adam and Eve simply understood God to be telling them *to fill* the earth for the first time and not *to refill* the world. They would absolutely not infer from God's command that there had been a world gone bad prior to theirs. In fact, there are no words or verses that support such a claim.[43]

9-The Day God Created Dinosaurs

All of the evidence that we have seen thus far has strongly supported a literal, six-day creation. We have examined the language of the Hebrew Bible (Old Testament) and scrutinized the ancient commentators and have seen only evidence pointing to the six days of creation as being 24-hour days, which, according to the Church Fathers and Jewish sources, occurred approximately six thousand to ten thousand years ago. Holding to a literal interpretation of Genesis and accepting the record of the dinosaurs, however, would seem to be diametrically opposed. According to evolutionary timescales, the dinosaurs lived hundreds of millions of years ago and died out about sixty-five million years ago. Therefore what are we to do with the dinosaurs if we also hold to a literal, six-day creation only several thousand years ago?

Dinosaurs Were Real

Some believers in the inerrancy of the Bible have simply dismissed the dinosaurs as having never existed almost as a knee-jerk-reaction to the controversy concerning the supposed *missing links* of human ancestry.[44] The collection of dinosaur bones, however, is a completely different question from that of man's supposed early ancestors, and hence their existence should not be in question.

The number of dinosaur bones that has been discovered is staggering. They have been found all over the world in large quantities, and sometimes entire skeletons have been found intact. There should be no doubt among young earth creationists that dinosaurs were real creatures that existed in great quantities in the past. The big question at hand is: *when* did they exist? The Bible-believing adherents of an old earth see the reality of dinosaurs as one more reason that evolutionary timescales must be true and must have taken place over millions of years. Indeed, we have been told so many times that dinosaurs died out around sixty-five millions years ago, that men and dinosaurs never coexisted, and that holding to a literal creation of six, 24-hour days of creation a few thousand years ago would seem to pose some problems. It is only a problem, however, until we realize that the Bible actually speaks of dinosaurs being created during the first six days and coexisting with men.

Where Are the Dinosaurs in the Bible?

So just where in the Bible are dinosaurs mentioned? The word *dinosaur*, per se, is never mentioned in the Bible. The word was not coined until 1841, twenty years after a British doctor, Dr. Mantell, discovered some teeth and bones in a quarry. They were so different from the bones and teeth of known lizards that they were eventually given a new name by another British scientist, Dr. Owen, who called them *dinosaurs,* meaning *terrible lizards*. Given that the name itself was not coined until the 1800s, we would not expect to find it in the Bible as such. But that does not mean that the Bible doesn't mention them by another name.

There are, in fact, dozens of verses that speak of dinosaurs sometimes as actual living physical creatures and sometimes as either physical or symbolic creatures.[45] We will look at the three main words in Hebrew, תנינם *tanninim,* בהמות *behemoth,* and לויתן *Leviathan,* which designate dinosaurs of various types. Though there are other words such as *Rahab* and *nahash,* which some people suggest refer to dinosaurs, their designation as dinosaurs is speculative. Therefore, we will focus on the large number of strong examples that we already have to work with.

Tanninim

The first word, *tanninim*, is found in Genesis 1:21, the fifth day of creation: "So God created great sea creatures [תנינם *tanninim*] and every living thing that moves, with which the waters abounded, according to their kind, and every winged bird according to its kind. And God saw that it was good." The word *tanninim* appears twenty-seven times in the Hebrew Old Testament, twenty-one of which have been translated as dragon (or dragons) in the King James Version (KJV), three times as serpent (and serpents), once as monster, and twice as whale (and whales).[46] Thus, we don't actually see the word *dinosaur* written in the text of an English Bible, but it is lying below the surface in the original language. Just how are we to understand this word though? Is this word referring to *great whales* as the KJV translates it here or as *great sea creatures* or *great sea monsters* as we see in other versions? Is it simply understood in a generic sense of a big creature or more specifically as a dinosaur-dragon-type creature?

The Origin of the Word

The origin of the word is not absolutely certain. The most accepted Hebrew lexicon, *Brown Driver Briggs*, suggests the following meanings: 1) dragon, serpent, sea monster; 1a) dragon or dinosaur; 1b) sea or river monster; 1c) serpent, venomous snake, though it suggests that *tanninim* may be related to a more primitive root of *tan* meaning *to howl*, and hence, by implication, *jackal*. This latter suggestion is questioned by many scholars due to linguistic considerations. The *Dictionary of Deities and Demons in the Bible* states regarding the origin of this word:

> AARTUN has revived the proposal [...] that Tannin is derived from a geminate root TNN, "to smoke, ascension of smoke," leading to the Ugaritic "the dragon, (sea) monster, snake (stretching out/moving forward like smoke)" (Van Der Toorn et al 1999: 834).

Three-Root Letters

Semitic languages are fascinating in that (almost) every word consists of three-root letters that serve as the foundation of the word. By adding prefixes, suffixes, and changing the vowels, the application (and implication) of the word changes, but the essential meaning remains the same. This idea can be seen in English, although it is still slightly different, in some words like *save*, *savior*, and *salvation*. These three words are all related with the common meaning of *save*, though they obviously have different roles.

In Hebrew and all Semitic languages, there are three principal letters which give a word its essential meaning. *Tanninim* consists of the three-root letters *tav, nun, nun* or TNN. Just as there are Spanish, French, and Italian words that are practically the same (such as *gato, chat,* and *gatto,* respectively meaning *cat*), the same is true of Semitic languages where a word in one language can be almost identical to that in another language. Thus, to find that the root *TNN* appears with a similar meaning in an ancient language called Ugaritic, which was spoken around approximately 1400 BC in what is today Lebanon, greatly helps us narrow down the search for the meaning.

According to R. E. Whitaker, *A Concordance of the Ugaritic Literature*, the word appears eight times (Whitaker 1972: 619). Six of those are couched in mythological texts, and three of those are concerning *tunnanu,* the great sea monsters. J. C. L. Gibson translates a particular text as "In the sea are Arsh and *the dragon*" (Gibson 1977: 81). The *Dictionary of Deities and Demons in the Bible* notes that the ideogram, which is a type of written picture, for *tunnanu,* is that of a snake (Van Der Toorn et al 1999: 835). Thus comparing the Hebrew word *tanninim* with the Ugaritic, we find that the word was indeed related to a creature, though associated with the Ugaritic gods, that was, nonetheless, a type of aquatic dragon which may have also breathed fire.

Dragons in the Septuagint

We should also consider the testimony of the Septuagint, which is the Greek translation of the Hebrew Scriptures done in approximately 270 BC by Alexandrian Jews. Therein we can gain an insight into an ancient understanding of the word. The Septuagint translates the word in Genesis 1:21 as κητη (*kete*) which means *monster.* However, the majority of the occurrences of the word *tanninim* are translated as δρακων (*drakon*), which is the origin of the English word *dragon.* There are many references to dragons in Greek literature. They were snake-like monsters (though often with feet) that were guardians of important places; they were not merely whales. Hence, the Greek translation of the word points in the direction that this class of creatures that God created on the fifth day was indeed a dragon or, in modern language, a type of sea "dinosaur."[47]

Behemoth

The next word is *behemoth* found in Job 40:15. *Behemoth* is the plural of the feminine noun *behema*, which simply means *beast.* It is curious to note here that *behemoth*, though plural, takes a singular and masculine verb (in Hebrew the number and gender of nouns and verbs must agree) thereby signifying not beasts, but a specific type of creature. Thus, the word *behemoth* here is not just a plural form, but a completely different creature or beast.

God's Description of Behemoth

In this passage, God comes, per Job's request, to testify that He is altogether above man's understanding and challenges Job to consider His creations, "Look now at the behemoth, which I made along with you ..." (Job 40:15). Notice how God declares that He made the behemoth along with Job. But even more importantly is the command "look now"—a clear statement that this creature was created at the same time and apparently lived contemporarily with Job, or he would not have had a clue what God was talking about and certainly would not have been able to "look" at what God was talking about.[48] God then lists many of the attributes of this creature that we will look at to get the best picture possible of what kind of animal this truly was.

> Look now at the behemoth, which I made along with you;
> **He eats grass like an ox.**
> See now, his strength is in his hips,
> And his power is in his stomach muscles.
> He **moves his tail like a cedar;**
> The sinews of his thighs are tightly knit.
> His **bones are like beams of bronze,**
> His **ribs like bars of iron.**
> He is the first of the ways of God;
> Only He who made him can bring near His sword.
> Surely the mountains yield food for him,
> And all the beasts of the field play there.
> He lies under the lotus trees,
> In a covert of reeds and marsh.
> The lotus trees cover him with their shade;
> The willows by the brook surround him.
> Indeed the river may rage,
> Yet he is not disturbed;
> He is confident, though the Jordan gushes into his mouth,
> Though he takes it in his eyes,
> Or one pierces his nose with a snare (Job 40:15–24, emphasis mine).

God says that "He eats grass like an ox." To say that the creature is like an ox in the food it eats means that it is not an ox, but rather it is only similar in the way that they both eat grass. There have been three main explanations as to what known animal this could be: elephant, crocodile, or hippopotamus. Both elephants and hippos are known to eat grass, while crocodiles, on the other hand, eat only meat (frogs, insects, or larger animals), but never grass. We can safely conclude that this creature is not a crocodile just from its diet.

Elephant or Hippo?

Could it be either an elephant or a hippo? Thomas Aquinas, a Catholic theologian of the thirteenth century, suggested that *behemoth* is in fact an elephant (Jackson 2005). This animal could possibly be an elephant in that they both eat grass, but what about the other characteristics? Do they really fit those of an elephant? "See now, his strength is in his hips, and his power is in his stomach muscles" (Job 40:16). The strength of an elephant is in its trunk, shoulders, and head. Its hips and stomach, though not weak compared to ours, are certainly not its outstanding characteristics. God then continues describing the animal, "He moves his tail like a cedar ..." (Job 40:17).

Just how big is a cedar tree? According to one source, a Lebanon cedar tree (assuming that is what Job would have understood) typically grows to around 81 feet tall and 112 inches (9.33 ft) in diameter. The tail of an adult male elephant measures between seven to ten inches at the widest part! [49] And just what would it be like to wag a tail that is like a cedar? Obviously, anything that got in its path would experience serious devastation. Getting in the path of an elephant's tail might not smell great, but it probably would not do much harm. What can be said about the tail of an elephant is equally true of a hippopotamus—the tail is little more than a fly swatter!

It's a Tail and Nothing Else

Some have tried to suggest that the Hebrew word זנב (*zanav* tail) should in fact be translated as the male genital instead. This theory is nothing more than an attempt to draw attention away from the true issue that in this text the tail of this creature does not fit that of any normal everyday kind of creature. *Zanav* is used eleven times in the Hebrew Bible including this passage in Job. Every occurrence outside of Job refers to a tail whether it be an animal's literal tail or a figurative usage of what comes after and not before. Several of those times the word is further defined by the contrast with the head, leaving little doubt that a tail, and not a sexual organ, is being referred to.[50]

The Bones

Next God states what his bones are like. To take this passage literally means that we understand that the text suggests that the bones are *like* bronze and iron, although they are not made of those actual materials. Care must be given not to overlook those small but important words that allow us to interpret literally. Nevertheless, the picture is given that the bones of this creature were of immense strength, implying that the creature itself was extremely big to need such strong bones. Although one could argue that elephants and hippos possess such strong bones, it would fit well in describing the strength of dinosaur bones, too. In fact, considering that "the weight of Brachiosaurus, the largest plant-eating dinosaur, is 50 metric tons," according to the Indian Institute of Astrophysics website, which is 49.2 English tons, its bones would have to be extremely strong. An adult male African elephant, the largest of all elephants, weighs in at 6.8 tons. While we should certainly not want it to step on our feet, it is much, much lighter than the heaviest of dinosaurs. The Brachiosaurus is seven times heavier than the elephant. The implications of such enormous size are summarized as follows:

> Galileo was the first to address the problem of support faced by land animals in the early 1600s. He theorized about the relation of size to strength and structure. Consider two animals of different sizes that are geometrically similar. If the larger is twice as long as the smaller animal, it is also twice as wide and twice as high. The larger creature outweighs its smaller counterpart eight times. Although the volume is eight times larger, the strength of its legs increases only by a factor of four. Thus, eight times the weight would have to be carried by only four times the bone strength. If an animal becomes progressively bigger without changing its shape, it must eventually reach a size at which it is incapable of supporting itself (Indian Institute of Astrophysics 2006).

While the above explanation does not consider the elephant and the Brachiosaurus specifically, the principle holds true that the bones of the dinosaur would have needed to be extremely strong to support such an enormous creature. Thus, the Bible's description of the bones being like bronze and iron is in no way an exaggeration if the animal were indeed a large dinosaur such as the Brachiosaurus. In fact, it would seem that no other creature except such a giant would merit the description of having bones like bronze and iron.

Leviathan

After questioning Job about his knowledge of Behemoth, God then continues to challenge him regarding another creature, whose description has caused many to dismiss it as purely myth. *The Dictionary of Deities and Demons in the Bible* states, "Obviously the author of Job 41 had access to some animal mythological literature relating to the Egyptian tradition" (Van Der Toorn et al 1999: 513). The author matter-of-factly states that the biblical writer, whom I believe to be Job, borrowed the tradition from another culture. The author of the dictionary has effectively declared that it was not God who spoke those words to Job, but rather some unknown author who was inspired by another culture.

A Dragon/Snake-Like Creature

A root similar to Leviathan is found in an Ugaritic text[51]— *litanu* whose etymology is thought to be either *"the twisting one* (cf. Arabic *lawiya*) or *the wreath-like, the circular* (cf. Heb *liwya*), both possibilities pointing to an original concept of Leviathan as a snake-like being" (Van Der Toorn et al 1999: 511). Other than this connection, no other supporting evidence is given to substantiate the claim that Job, or whoever is believed to have written the biblical book of Job, borrowed the idea from others rather than being told divinely by God Himself. Most Ugaritic texts are from the fifteenth century BC, although many believe that the book of Job is much older than that. Granted, the date of Job is controversial and not altogether certain. However, if the early date of Job is accepted, then it is at least possible that the account in Job is the original, while the Ugaritic account is merely a distortion of it. Although we may not be able to prove conclusively which account is older, we can look at the Bible's own description of this amazing creature.

God's Description of Leviathan

We are told in Isaiah 27:1 that at that point God will "punish Leviathan the fleeing serpent, Leviathan that twisted serpent; and He will slay the reptile that is in the sea." Due to the end-times nature of this passage, it cannot be ruled out that this may be metaphorical language referring to Satan who is called the dragon of old in Revelation 12:9. On the other hand, we are told specifically that the creature lives in the sea and is some type of twisting serpent-like creature as we saw in the Ugaritic text.

Psalm 104, verses 26 and 27, provides an important natural-istic description of Leviathan indicating that it was a real, his-torical creature as far as the Bible is concerned. "There the ships sail about; there is that Leviathan which You have made to play there. These all wait for You, that You may give them their food in due season." The fact that Leviathan lives where the ships sail and is listed with the innumerable teeming things which live in the sea (Psalm 104:25) strongly demonstrates that, whatever it was, it was one of the many creatures that God made. The detailed description of Leviathan is given in Job 41 where God challenges Job if he is able to contend with Leviathan, with the implication that God alone is able.

> Can you draw out Leviathan with a hook,
> Or snare his tongue with a line which you lower?
> Can you put a reed through his nose,
> Or pierce his jaw with a hook?
> Will he make many supplications to you?
> Will he speak softly to you?
> Will he make a covenant with you?
> Will you take him as a servant forever?

Will you play with him as with a bird,
Or will you leash him for your maidens?
Will your companions make a banquet of him?
Will they apportion him among the merchants? (Job
41:1–6).

Not an Ordinary Creature!

God is stating in unambiguous terms that this creature is no ordinary creature. He is not some animal that one can tame like the other animals and is not one that is taken as food for a banquet (verse 6). God then goes on to describe how this creature is practically invincible because no spear can pierce him and his entire body is covered with a type of armor impenetrable to man's weapons.

Can you fill his skin with harpoons,
Or his head with fishing spears?
Lay your hand on him;
Remember the battle—never do it again!
Indeed, any hope of overcoming him is false;
Shall one not be overwhelmed at the sight of him?
No one is so fierce that he would dare stir him up (Job
41:7–10).

Invincible

The description that God gives of this creature is remarkable. There is no known animal on the entire earth that was so fierce that man could not conquer it. God declares that because no one would dare stir Leviathan up that there was no one who was able to stand against God. No elephant, hippopotamus, crocodile, or any other creature is invincible to man. Although many men may die fighting, given enough spears and men, every creature would eventually fall at the hands of men—with the exception of one. This creature can be conquered by God alone. God continues describing Leviathan.

I will not conceal his limbs,
His mighty power, or his graceful proportions.

> Who can remove his outer coat?
> Who can approach him with a double bridle?
> Who can open the doors of his face,
> With his terrible teeth all around?
> His rows of scales are his pride,
> Shut up tightly as with a seal;
> One is so near another
> That no air can come between them;
> They are joined one to another,
> They stick together and cannot be parted (Job 41:12–17).

Some remarkable traits of Leviathan are his terrible teeth, true of the crocodile but certainly not of the elephant or hippopotamus. The teeth is where the similarity to the crocodile ends, however, for Leviathan has an outer coat which none can remove and has rows of scales which no air can come between nor can they be parted. It is true that crocodiles have a hard and scaly backside, but their belly is soft and vulnerable. In verse 30 we are told that his undersides are sharp and that he leaves marks in the mire—characteristics hardly true of the crocodile.

Fire-Breathing

What is truly shocking about Leviathan is that God states that he breathed fire.

> His sneezings flash forth light,
> And his eyes are like the eyelids of the morning.
> Out of his mouth go burning lights;
> Sparks of fire shoot out.
> Smoke goes out of his nostrils,
> As from a boiling pot and burning rushes.
> His breath kindles coals,
> And a flame goes out of his mouth (Job 41:18–21).

I admit that when I first contemplated the thought of a fire-breathing dragon as actually being real, I was skeptical. But then I began to consider it and eventually came to the conclusion:

why not? After all, fireflies are tiny creatures that produce something inside of them that produces light as do numerous bioluminescent marine animals including the electric eel. Certainly an amazing creature is the bombardier beetle, which, when being attacked by a predator, can release chemicals in its rear to provide about seventy quick explosions which are fatal to other insects. Thus, if a little beetle is able to create an explosion from its tiny body, who is to say that dinosaurs might not also have been able to breathe fire? Perhaps the legends of fire-breathing dragons from all over the world actually hold some validity.

A Shining Wake

God then finishes by giving some other characteristics of Leviathan that separate him from all other creatures, especially any of the animals living today. He could swim so rapidly and above the surface of the water that he left a shining wake, making people think that the "deep had white hair!" In God's words, there is nothing like him on earth and so ... he is king over all the children of pride" (verse 34):

> Strength dwells in his neck,
> And sorrow dances before him.
> The folds of his flesh are joined together;
> They are firm on him and cannot be moved.
> His heart is as hard as stone,
> Even as hard as the lower millstone.
> When he raises himself up, the mighty are afraid;
> Because of his crashings they are beside themselves.
> Though the sword reaches him, it cannot avail;
> Nor does spear, dart, or javelin.
> He regards iron as straw,
> And bronze as rotten wood.
> The arrow cannot make him flee;
> Slingstones become like stubble to him.
> Darts are regarded as straw;
> He laughs at the threat of javelins.

His undersides are like sharp potsherds;
He spreads pointed marks in the mire.
He makes the deep boil like a pot;
He makes the sea like a pot of ointment.
He leaves a shining wake behind him;
One would think the deep had white hair.
On earth there is nothing like him,
Which is made without fear.
He beholds every high thing;
He is king over all the children of pride (Job
41:22–34).

Impenetrable Armor

Anna Gosline, writing for the NewScientist.com news service, writes about the amazing body armor of one type of dinosaur known as Ankylosaurs, which, though it is not to be equated with Leviathan, does provide an excellent example of what these impenetrable scales may have been like—pointing to the veracity of the account in Job 41.

An in-depth study of dinosaur armor has revealed an unexpected new level of strength, with some plates having a weave of fibers resembling today's bullet-proof fabrics. The likely strength of such plates makes the dinosaurs studied—Ankylosaurs—perhaps the best—protected creatures to have ever stalked the Earth [...] Ankylosaurs were massive herbivores that grew up to 10 meters in length during the late Jurassic and Cretaceous periods. The coin-sized plates sported by the Ankylosaurs fully covered their back, neck, head and even protected their eyes [...] They had sets of structural fibers running parallel and perpendicular to the surface, and then further sets at forty-five degrees to each of these axes, providing strength in all directions. The fibers of the bulletproof fabric Kevlar are similarly arranged (Gosline 2004).

Where Is the Proof?

So the Bible does in fact claim that men and dinosaurs once lived together. However, there is still so much research regarding dinosaurs and so many experts attest that they died out about sixty-five million years ago. If the dinosaurs really did exist with men as the Bible claims, shouldn't we see some proof of that other than mere oral accounts that many believe are suspect to exaggeration and mythologizing? Wouldn't we expect to see some hard facts substantiating men and dinosaurs living together?

Soft Tissue and Red Blood Cells

The evidence that men and dinosaurs coexisted not millions of years ago but only thousands of years ago lies right in front of our faces; but out of fear, most refuse to see. The evidence of Job and the description of two dinosaurs is evidence not to be lightly brushed off; nevertheless, it remains invisible to many. The discovery of soft tissue complete with blood vessels in dinosaur bones should be just such evidence that should make people reconsider their paradigm. Dr. Schweitzer, who made the discovery, even suggested, "We may not really know as much about how fossils are preserved as we think" (Peake 2005). Dr. Carl Wieland remarks regarding the discovery:

> One description of a portion of the tissue was that it is "flexible and resilient and when stretched returns to its original shape." Dr. Schweitzer ... has been cited as saying that the blood vessels were flexible, and that in some instances, one could squeeze out their contents. Furthermore, she said, "The microstructures that look like cells are preserved in every way." She also is reported as commenting that "preservation of this extent, where you still have this flexibility and transparency, has never been seen in a dinosaur before."
>
> The reason that this possibility has long been overlooked seems obvious: the overriding belief in "millions of years." The long-age paradigm (dominant

belief system) blinded researchers to the possibility, as it were. It is inconceivable that such things should be preserved for (in this case) "seventy million years."

Unfortunately, the long-age paradigm is *so* dominant that facts alone will not readily overturn it. As philosopher of science Thomas Kuhn pointed out, **what generally happens when a discovery contradicts a paradigm is that the paradigm is not discarded but modified, usually by making secondary assumptions, to accommodate the new evidence.**

That's just what appears to have happened in this case. When Schweitzer first found what appeared to be blood cells in a *T. Rex* specimen, she said, **"It was exactly like looking at a slice of modern bone. But, of course, I couldn't believe it. I said to the lab technician: "The bones, after all, are sixty-five million years old. How could blood cells survive that long?"'** Notice that her first reaction was to question the evidence, not the paradigm (Wieland 2005, emphasis mine).

Dinosaur tissue is an amazing challenge to the old-earth paradigm, but it still doesn't prove that men and dinosaurs coexisted as the Bible clearly claims. However, evidence that men and dinosaurs lived together in the past does exist and is available for scrutiny to all who are willing to reconsider the paradigm. Let's now consider some archaeological evidence that men and dinosaurs lived together.

10-The Day Men Saw Dinosaurs

[The] co-occurrence of men and dinosaurs [...] would dispel an earth with vast antiquity. The entire history of creation, including the day of rest, could be accommodated in the seven biblical days of the Genesis myth. Evolution would be vanquished (Louis Jacobs, 1993: 261, Former President of the Society of Vertebrate Paleontology).

Challenging the Paradigm

In the country of Peru during the 1960s, after the collapse of a cave during a flood, some surprisingly strange stones were found. Carved on the stones are depictions of advanced technology such as men looking through telescopes, some type of brain surgery, and what appears to be open-heart surgery. There are also numerous stones of creatures that have every appearance of dinosaurs.

There are a few different reactions to these stones. Dr. Javier Cabrera, who collected approximately eleven thousand stones, postulated that the carvings were evidence of an advanced, ancient civilization that lived at the time of dinosaurs (over sixty-five millions years ago). Erich von Daniken, in his book *Chariots of the Gods*, saw the stones as evidence that the earth had been visited in ages past by extraterrestrial beings.

Most often, however, the stones are routinely dismissed as forgeries[52] because of the advanced technology on them and especially because they have drawings on them of men interacting with creatures that modern science claims lived and died out millions of years ago.

Needed Skepticism

Dennis Swift is one of the foremost experts today on what have become known as the Ica Stones, named after the valley in which they were found. In his book, *Secrets of the Ica Stones and Nazca Lines*, he documents the vast collection of stones after making several trips there with geologist Dr. Patton and visiting with Dr. Cabrera. The current estimate of the number of stones is well over fifteen thousand.

Obviously, the discovery of the stones has been met with much skepticism—and justifiably so. People have, in the past, resorted to creating archaeological forgeries and fakes in order to make the latest and greatest discovery. One such example was performed by renowned archeologist Dr. Fujimura, who was caught in November of 2000 planting stone tools in an archeological dig site (Yamada 2002). Although the actions of Dr. Fujimura cannot be said to be standard procedure for archeologists and paleontologists, this was not the first time that hoaxes have been performed in order to strengthen the accepted paradigm of evolution.[53]

Challenging the evidence is a good thing whenever a new theory is presented. The Ica Stones and other such discoveries are no exception. Nevertheless, let's weigh the evidence and see if these stones merit our attention.

Mentioned in Historical Documents

They were first mentioned in the 1500s by Spanish explorers as noted by the Indian chronicler Juan de Santa Cruz Pachachuti Llamgui, who wrote:

> At the time of the Peru-tomb Pachachuti many carved stones were found in the Kingdom of Chperu-tomb

[...] It is noted that some of these stones were taken back to Spain. The chronicler of the Peru-tombs wrote in about 1570. The OJO, Lima Domingo, a major newspaper in Lima, Peru, on October 3, 1993, described a Spanish Priest traveling in the area of Ica in 1525 inquiring about the unusual engraved stones with strange animals on them (Patton 2006).

Nazca Graves

The Ica Valley, where the stones have been found, is the ancient seat of the Nazca people who left thousands of graves filled with numerous artifacts such as textiles, pottery, and these curious stones as well.

The climate of the valley is similar to Egypt in that it is extremely arid and can receive no rain for years on end, which, on the upside, is ideal for preserving ancient artifacts. The stones range in size from a few ounces up to one thousand pounds. To date, over fifteen thousand have been found. Dr. Swift notes concerning the stones' depictions that they have "carvings of dinosaurs such as Stegosaurus, Diplodocus, Pterodactyls, Triceratops ,and Apatosaurs. What is absolutely incredible are the carvings showing men riding or fighting dinosaurs" (Swift 2005: 16).

Picture 1 Nazca Tomb: Tombs in the deserts of Peru often preserve amazing artifacts which are very old, including the beautiful, intricate textiles of the Nazca culture (ca. 700 AD).

Sophisticated Drawings

The drawings are neither crude nor unsophisticated in their depiction of dinosaurs. In fact, some demonstrate specific details about dinosaurs such as the composition of their skin and other features, which have only recently been discovered by paleontologists.

Picture 2 Peruvian Textiles: These textiles depict living dinosaurs.

Picture 3 Tomb Pottery: This pottery is on display at the Rafael Laredo Herrera Museum in Lima, Peru.

Dr. Swift made comments after reviewing the photos taken on his 1967 trip to Peru and his visit to Dr. Cabrera who holds the collection of eleven thousand stones. He notes that on one of the stones was the depiction of a Brontosaurus with a long skull. Only in 1979 did two researchers from the Carnegie Museum discover that the Brontosaurus in the museum at the time had the wrong head:

> Brontosaurus today is known as Apatosaurus because that was the name given to a skeleton found in 1877. Apatosaurs had a heavy body and heavy legs, a long head, long neck, and long tail. Apatosaurus means deceptive reptile, but it was O. C. Marsh who was deceptive in not reporting where he got the skull that he put on the dinosaur skeleton. The fact that the Cabrera Collection has stones dug up in the 1950s and '60s from Peruvian tombs dating up to two thousand four hundred years old with Apatosaurus dinosaurs on them lends some credence to their authenticity. **If the stones were a hoax would not the artist have relied upon dinosaur books, movies, or science journals of the 1940s to 1960s vintage?** Then why don't the dinosaurs on the stones have the wrong head? (Swift 2005: 49, emphasis mine).

Possible Hoaxes?

Still, couldn't they be frauds planted by overzealous devotees seeking to prove that men and dinosaurs lived together? Or could they not be forgeries made to sell tourists? Consider the following evidence that rules out the possibility of them being an elaborate hoax.

The sheer number of stones is simply impossible for a few peasants to produce in the past forty years. Fifteen thousand (plus) stones (some weighing up to one thousand pounds) represent an astronomical amount of labor which would take more than a lifetime for one person to perform.

One estimate put the total time to carve all the stones at 375,000 working hours. That would be 12 hours a day, seven days a week for about 85 years! Only two modern-day Peruvians, Basilio and Irma, claim to have carved any stones. It seems impossible for them to have had the time to carve all fifteen thousand stones (Bermingham 2006).

Picture 4 Allosauruses Attacking Man.

There is very little incentive to produce so many since the stones were sold extremely cheaply compared to the necessary labor involved (minimum 12–15 hours to produce a small one). Feeding one's family from carving these to sell to the tourists would amount to very little.

Furthermore, the quality of the artwork of the known to be fake stones carved by Basilio was not nearly as sophisticated as that seen on the authentic stones found in graves. The stones demonstrate an advanced knowledge of medicine such as some type of brain surgery (see Picture 5), which has later been corroborated with the discovery of skulls that showed signs of recovery from surgery. We know that the patients lived for a fair amount of time after the surgery since the skulls show that the bone (over a shell plate) around the incision had time to grow back—something that doesn't happen if the patient dies right away! Additionally, evidence of knowledge of technologies that were once thought to only be common to modern man has been seen on the stones, such as telescopes and even hot air balloons. Thus, the stones do not represent the work of simple peasants.

Picture 5 Ancient Brain Surgery?

Expert Analysis

Research concerning the Ica Stones has involved various experts who have expressed their opinion and findings that the stones are authentic and genuine; they are not fakes. One such expert is Colonel Omar Chioino Carraza, who in 1974 was the director of the Peruvian Aeronautical Museum. He expressed his belief in the authenticity of the stones after the government conducted official tests.

> It seems certain to me [...] that they are a message
> from a very ancient people whose memory has been

lost to history. They were engraved several thousand years ago. They've been known in Peru for a long time and my museum has more than four hundred of them (Swift 2004).

Picture 6 Man and Diplodocus (Sauropod): Sauropod frills were discovered in 1992, yet they were being drawn correctly 2,000 years ago.

Swift points out "The National Aeronautical Museum's collection of engraved stones including dinosaurs was acquired from various locations throughout Peru" (Swift 2004). He also notes the testimony of Pablo Soldi, who found a large collection of stones with his brother, "A thick layer of saltpeter covering the main specimens could only be explained by the passage of considerable time" (Swift 2004). Furthermore, Archaeologist Alejandro Pezzia Asserto from the National Archaeology Department of Peru,

> ... who was in charge of archaeological investigations in the cultural province of Ica and a trustee of the Ica Museum, conducted official excavations in the ancient Paracas and Ica cemeteries of Max Uhle and Toma Luz. **On two separate occasions, engraved stones were excavated from pre-Hispanic Indian tombs**

dating from 400 BC to 700 AD. The engraved stones were embedded in the side of the mortuary chamber of the tombs and next to mummies. **Alejandro Pezzia Asserto published his work with drawings and descriptions of the stones with a five-toed llama that was supposed to be extinct for over forty million years.** Other stones were of a **fish that allegedly had been extinct for over 100 million years** and a bird in flight. These stones became the possession of the Ica Museum as part of the Colca Collection (Swift 2004, emphasis mine).

The Rocks in the Laboratory

Dr. Swift commissioned a local man, Basilio, who was known to have sold stones occasionally, to carve one in order to test it against one that Dr. Swift found in an actual Nazca grave and one from Dr. Cabrera's collection. It was easy to see that Basilio's was a fake. Under the microscope, evidence of metal instruments could be seen; there was no patina or film of oxidation, saltpeter, or microorganisms.

On the other hand, the one from Dr. Cabrera's collection had no evidence of metal tools being used, dirt and sand were in the cracks, and natural oxidization was evident. There was a heavy coat of patina all over the rocks as well as microorganisms in the grooves. The conclusion from the Mason Optical Laboratory regarding the Cabrera rock was that the rock was not recent but rather old (Swift 2005: 69).

The rock found by Dr. Swift *in situ* at a cave in Nazca tomb at Rio Grande had a similar analysis: it had a heavy coat of patination, microorganisms in the grooves, saltpeter, lichen growth on one section, and even an apparent blood stain over the dinosaur image. **"The salient conclusion of the laboratory is that the stone is of some age: in fact, of antiquity of hundreds or thousands of years old"** (Swift 2005: 71).

Dr. Swift later took the stones to another laboratory, Palm Abrasive Company in Oregon, suspecting that skeptics might question the analysis of the findings of only one laboratory. They used an ROI optical video that delivers zoom microscopical viewing in the 20x to 500x range. The coordinate measuring machine attached to it positions resolution to better than fifty millionths of an inch. Palm Abrasive found the same features as before. In fact, the apparent blood stain they noted was "characteristic of that found on textiles and ceramics that are interred with mummies" (Swift 2004). Thus to suggest that the stones are fakes is due to bias, not the evidence from the laboratory.

The Ica Stones Are Not Unique

The evidence of the Ica Stones is not unique. In fact, there are carvings and figurines from around the world which show that the artists must have seen a living dinosaur from time to time.

Picture 7 Natural Bridges National Park, Utah: The park literature attributes the petroglyphs to the Anasazi who inhabited the area from approximately 400 AD to 1300 AD.

Acambaro, Mexico Figurines

In 1945, Waldemar Julsrud discovered a collection of twenty thousand or more ceramic figurines in the village of Acambaro (a few hundred miles from Guadalajara), Mexico which, unlike the Ica Stones, can be dated easily and with a fair amount of accuracy since they are made of clay. The figurines (See Picture 8) most likely originated from the Chupicauro civilization that flourished from approximately 500 BC to 500 AD. This amazing collection contains at least twenty-three known types of dinosaurs and others that are still unknown.

Because thousands of figurines strongly suggest that ancient man actually saw living dinosaurs, the discovery was quickly claimed to be a hoax. Dr. Swift notes the measures taken to determine conclusively that the figurines were not a hoax as claimed, but are in fact authentic:

> In 1955 Charles Hapgood, respected Professor of Anthropology at the University of New Hampshire, conducted an elaborate investigation including extensive radiometric dating. He was accompanied by Earl Stanley Gardner, former District Attorney of the city of Los Angeles, California, and the creator of Perry Mason. They falsified the claim that Julsrud manufactured the figurines by excavating under the house of the Chief of Police, which was built 25 years before Julsrud arrived in Mexico. Forty-three more examples of the same type were found. Three radiocarbon tests were performed by Isotopes Incorporated of New Jersey resulting in dates of **1640 BC, 4530 BC, and 1110 BC**. Eighteen samples were subjected to thermo luminescent testing by the University of Pennsylvania, **all of which gave dates of approximately 2500 BC**. These results were subsequently withdrawn when it was learned that some of the samples were from dinosaurs (Swift 2006, emphasis mine).

Picture 8 Acambaro Dinosaur Figurine.

Carving in Cambodia

In January of 2006, Drs. Patton and Swift journeyed to Cambodia to the temple monastery, Ta Prohm. The temple was built by Jayavarman VII in honor of his mother and dedicated in 1186 AD (see Picture 9 Temple Monastery Ta Prohm). The walls of the monastery were decorated with hundreds of kinds of animals, one of which was a creature that closely resembles a Stegosaurus. Drs. Patton and Swift note that the likeness of a Stegosaurus has also been observed by two magazines. One of the magazines states, "Along the vertical strip of roundels in the angle between the south wall of the porch and the east wall of the main body of the *gopura* there is even a very convincing representation of a Stegosaur" (*Ancient Angor* 1999).[54]

Picture 9 Temple Monastery Ta Prohm.

Picture 10 Stegosaurus-Looking Creature.

Three Possible Answers

Thus, we are left with essentially three possibilities regarding the evidence showing men and dinosaurs together. The first is that man and dinosaurs actually lived together sixty-five (plus) million years ago. This, of course, is unacceptable to the evolutionary model and is obviously contradictory to the belief in a recent, literal, six-day creation. The second possibility is that dinosaurs did not die out sixty-five million years ago, but rather continued until the time of early man one million years ago according to the evolutionary timescale. The third is simply that man and dinosaurs lived together in the relatively near past (less than ten thousand years ago). None of these options is very acceptable to evolutionists; but the evidence that men and dinosaurs coexisted is ample though it is only visible to those willing to see.

This selective vision caused by the evolutionary paradigm has prevented many people from reaching the conclusion that dinosaurs (etc.) did not die out millions and millions of years ago—in spite of continual discoveries of living species thought to have died out millions of years ago. In 1938, a fish, the Coelacanth, which was believed to have died out with the dinosaurs, was discovered as still living. Keith S. Thomson, executive officer, Academy of Natural Sciences states that:

> Off the coast of southern Africa, in the winter of 1938, a fishing boat called *The Nerine* dragged from the Indian Ocean near the Chalumna River **a fish thought to be extinct for 70 million years.** The fish was a coelacanth, **an animal that thrived concurrently with dinosaurs** (Thompson 1991 book cover, emphasis mine).

Thompson also notes concerning the Dawn Redwood that it was "thought to be extinct worldwide until living specimens were found in central China in 1945" (Thompson 1991: 72).

A similar example is in a 1994 article entitled: "Newfound Pine Goes Back in Time—It was Believed to be Extinct." The tree was thought to have been extinct for one hundred million years.

David Noble was out on a holiday hike when he stepped off the beaten path and into the prehistoric age. Venturing into an isolated grove in a rain-forest preserve 125 miles from Sydney, the Parks and Wildlife service officer suddenly found himself in a real-life 'Jurassic Park'—standing amid trees thought to have disappeared 150 million years ago. "**The discovery is the equivalent of finding a small dinosaur still alive on earth**," said Carrick Chambers, director of the Royal Botanic Gardens. "The biggest tree towers 180 feet with a 10-foot girth, indicating that it is at least 150 years old. The trees are covered in dense, waxy foliage and have a knobby bark that makes them look like they are coated with bubbly chocolate."

Barbara Briggs, the botanic gardens' scientific director, hailed the find as one of Australia's most outstanding discoveries of the century [...] "The closest relatives of the Wollemi Pines died out in the Jurassic Period, 190 million to 135 million years ago, and the Cretaceous Period, 140 million to 65 million years ago" (*Salt Lake City Tribune*, December 15, 1994, p. A10, from *Associated Press*, emphasis mine).

All three examples are *surprise* discoveries merely because the billions of years of evolution are considered to be an established (and uncontestable) fact. Fish and trees thought to have coexisted (and died out) with the dinosaurs have been found to still exist. Perhaps there is so much surprise because the paradigm of when the dinosaurs lived and died out is wrong. We saw that the Bible plainly talks about dinosaurs under names such as *Tanninim*, *Behemoth*, and *Leviathan*. According to the Bible, God created dinosaurs during the first six days along with man. If we read the first six days in Genesis as literal days, we are not surprised by such discoveries; we anticipate them and are strengthened by them. Furthermore, men and dinosaurs carved on stones are not a problem, but a simple confirmation of what God has already revealed.

11-Are Six Days Enough?

If we truly affirm that God made the heavens and the earth in six literal days several thousand years ago, we are forced to consider four questions that have a direct association with such a worldview. If the heavens and the earth are young, then: (1) How could light from the edges of the universe, which is estimated to be 15 billion light years away, be here now? (2) Why does radioisotope dating seem to point to the vast majority of the earth's rocks being many billions of years old? (3) How do we account for the many layers of strata in places like the Grand Canyon indicating that it was formed over millions of years? (4) What about many fossils in the geologic column which are claimed to prove millions of years of evolution? We will very briefly touch upon these enormous areas of study just to see that there are very plausible answers from a literal, six-day creationist perspective.

These four questions have essentially served as the foundation of the evolutionary timescale and provide a dilemma for all who hold the Bible as God's Word. A solution popularized by Dr. Hugh Ross is to set up the witness of creation on a par with God's written Word. He says,

> God's revelation is not limited exclusively to the Bible's words. The facts of nature may be likened to a sixty-seventh book of the Bible. Just as we rightfully expect interpretations of Isaiah to be consistent with those of Mark, so too we can expect interpretations of the facts

of nature to be consistent with the messages of Genesis and the rest of the Canon.

Some readers might fear I am implying that God's revelation through nature is somehow on an equal footing with His revelation through the words of the Bible. Let me simply state that truth, by definition, is information that is perfectly free of contradiction and error. Just as it is absurd to speak of some entity as more perfect than another, so also one revelation of God's truth cannot be held as inferior or superior to another (Ross 1994: 56–57).

Dr. Ross is of course correct in that we expect the facts of nature to be consistent with Scripture. The problem, however, is not with the revelation of nature as a testament of God's power. Indeed, Psalm 19:1 even supports such a statement: "The heavens declare the glory of God; and the firmament shows His handiwork." Paul in the book of Romans (1:20) adds decisively "For since the creation of the world His invisible attributes are clearly seen, being understood by the things that are made, even His eternal power and Godhead, so that they are without excuse." There is no conflict between the Bible and nature, but rather with man's interpretation of nature and the Bible. God's general revelation of nature correctly interpreted is always 100 percent consistent with God's written revelation the Bible.

Dr. Ross is assuming that the evolutionary paradigm is the correct interpretation of nature. He has failed to mention that many of the theories that have provided us with ages of the earth and the universe are based on the evolutionary belief that there is no God. He has also erred because the Bible never changes. The truths contained therein never change and have withstood the testing of skeptics and critics for over two thousand years. However, man's interpretation of the world around him has done nothing but change as long as man has kept history. By making creation the sixty-seventh book of the Bible by which we can interpret the Bible, he is requiring man's interpretation of nature (with all of our biases and incomplete knowledge) to be the judge of the Bible. Rather, we need to let nature be subject to the interpretation of the Bible, for only then will the correct interpretation be obtained.

Starlight and Time

The question of how could light from fifteen billion light years away arrive in just six days has been taken up by Dr. Russell Humphreys. In his book, *Starlight and Time* (2004), he proposes an answer to the seemingly unsolvable enigma. The foundation of his theory lies in the fact that we know for certain that clocks change based on how close one is to a strong gravitational field or potential. He points out that the atomic clock in Greenwich, England, which is at sea level, ticks five microseconds slower per year than an identical clock in Boulder, Colorado (Humphreys 2004: 12). Because the clock in Boulder is approximately one mile higher in altitude than its counterpart in Greenwich, it ticks five microseconds per year faster. The Boulder clock is further away from the center of the earth, approximately the center of gravity, and is in a weaker gravitational field as a result. Dr. Stan Sholar, a retired aerospace scientist, confirms the reality of this phenomenon:

> One should make a distinction between the rate of passage of time and the behavior of clocks, or anything that measures time. If we define time as behavior of clocks then this distinction disappears. Einstein's theory of Special Relativity shows that lengths change with velocity, and clocks, whether pendulums or atomic, respond to such, but also to gravity. For clocks in GPS satellites, we have to correct for the slightly non-circular orbits where velocity and altitude vary continuously.
>
> For example, near apogee (the greatest distance from earth), the slower velocity causes the clock to run faster, due to Special Relativity. Also here there is a General

Relativity effect due to the higher gravitational potential (though lower force) causing the clock to run even faster at the higher altitude. The point being that it is actually an even more profound example because of the fact that the clocks on orbit are much higher than Boulder, Colorado, and relative to Greenwich (Sholar, personal communication, September 23, 2006).

Thus, just here on earth we find concrete evidence that the measurement of time's rate of passing changes according to the proximity of the clocks to a strong gravitational field, as approximately indicated by proximity to the earth's center of gravity. Humphreys then notes that the mathematics demonstrate that while the earth's clock was ticking at what he coins "Earth Standard Time" the clock in the outer parts of the universe was ticking faster and hence "the light has ample time *in the extra-terrestrial reference frame* to travel the required distances" (Humphreys 2004: 13).

I spoke personally with Dr. Humphreys at a conference in Anaheim, California, in February of 2005 after hearing him present his theory. After sharing with him how much I liked his theory, he humbly replied that his was not the final answer, but merely a plausible explanation. Dr. Humphreys presents a theory to solve such a difficult dilemma, but in the end, it is not the answer but a *plausible* explanation, which is satisfactory because none of us was there to witness exactly what techniques God used. Nevertheless, what is crucial to note is that there are scientifically plausible theories that support the biblical account without seeking to spiritualize, allegorize, or even dismiss the clear writing of the text.

The Rocks Speak

The other seemingly unsolvable enigma is that of radiometric dating of rocks yielding ages billions of years old. According to the popular definition of Wikipedia, "radiometric dating is a technique used to date materials based on a knowledge of the decay rates of naturally occurring isotopes, and the current abundances" (Wikipedia Radiometric Dating 2006). Since these decay rates occur extremely slowly, it is believed that the material being dated is of great antiquity. There are inherent problems involved with this method, thus not making it a failsafe method of dating rocks.[55] The work on polonium radiohalos by Dr. Gentry and the work on Zircon crystals by the RATE (Radioisotopes and the Age of the Earth) team strongly challenge the accepted assumptions involved with radiometric dating. In fact, their independent research has yielded some "rock solid" evidence that the earth is not billions of years old but only several thousand.

Polonium Radiohalos

Beginning in 1987, nuclear physicist Dr. Robert Gentry began examining discolorations in minerals. He has since examined over 100,000 of these "radiohalos" found in rocks, making his work the foundation of polonium halo research. He describes these "radiohalos:" "Etched within earth's foundation rocks (the granites) are beautiful microspheres of coloration, halos, produced by the radioactive decay of primordial polonium, which is known to have only a fleeting existence" (www.halos.com/index.htm).

An example analogous to Alka-Seltzer is given demonstrating the fleeting life of the radioactive polonium. It is this moment in which the radiohalos can be captured that yields proof to them having cooled instantaneously (during the time of the flood according to the RATE team, see below) rather than the supposed slow cooling of the earth suggested by evolution.

> A speck of polonium in molten rock can be compared to an Alka-Seltzer dropped into a glass of water. The beginning of effervescence is equated to the moment that polonium atoms began to emit radioactive particles. In molten rock the traces of those radioactive particles would disappear as quickly as the Alka-Seltzer bubbles in water. But if the water were instantly frozen,

the bubbles would be preserved. Likewise, polonium halos could have formed only if the rapidly "effervescing" specks of polonium had been instantly encased in solid rock.

An exceedingly large number of polonium halos are embedded in granites around the world. Just as frozen Alka-Seltzer bubbles would be clear evidence of the quick-freezing of the water, so are these many polonium halos undeniable evidence that a sea of primordial matter quickly "froze" into solid granite. The occurrence of these polonium halos, then, distinctly implies that our earth was formed in a very short time, in complete harmony with the biblical record of creation (www.halos.com/index.htm).

Radioisotopes and the Age of the Earth

An eight-year study began in 1997 that involved seven scientists with the primary goal of clarifying the chronology of the earth by studying, in particular, the properties of zircon crystals (similar to the work of Dr. Gentry with polonium). The research has now culminated in evidence strongly indicating that the earth is young. The seven scientists gave their research effort the acronym RATE, which stands for Radioisotopes and the Age of the Earth. The findings of their research are available in a two-volume set *Radioisotopes and the Age of the Earth*, in a layman's version (book and DVD) called *Thousands Not Billions* by Dr. Don DeYoung, who offers a partial summary of their research:

> RATE research obtained some of the first high-precision data on helium diffusion in zircon. A theoretical model based on this data gives an age for the earth of about 6,000 years. The presence of helium in zircons is a serious challenge to the concept of deep time. The helium also represents compelling evidence of accelerated nuclear decay in the past (DeYoung 2005: 176).

These and many more resources demonstrating that the apparent Achilles' heel of the Young Earth Creation model is not a fatal blow are available at the Institute for Creation Research's website (icr.org).

The findings of Dr. Gentry on polonium radiohalos and the RATE team on zircon crystals provide compelling evidence based on thorough investigation, experimentation, and observation that the earth is not billions of years old, but is rather *approximately* six thousand years old, thus implying that the creation week was six literal days.

The Grand Canyon and Mount St. Helens: Keys to Geology

Picture 11 Strata layers in the Grand Canyon (photograph by Anna Hamp).

The Grand Canyon is certainly one of the earth's most amazing places. It leaves us in awe of its size and beauty. There are, however, many questions that are raised in relation to it. The most central questions are how did it form and how long did the process take? The answer lies in looking primarily at the canyon walls. There are hundreds of thousands and even millions of layers also known as strata. These layers, when looking from the side, look like many pieces of cardboard stacked upon another. The accepted geological explanation for these strata is that each layer represents an annual or few years' cycle of deposition of minerals. Then the Colorado River (at its current rate) cut through the canyon exposing the strata that had already been laid down.

Therefore it is believed that since there are millions of strata, it must have taken hundreds of thousands or millions of years to form. Could there be, however, another plausible explanation for the almost innumerable layers?

Picture 12 Grand Canyon Clearly Defined Strata.

Cataclysmic Change

Picture 13 Little Grand Canyon, Mount St. Helens (photgraph by Douglas Hamp).

On May 18, 1980, scientists and tourists from all over the world witnessed an event that would provide a much better and almost inescapable model than the standard uniformitarianism model. In that year, Mount St. Helens in the state of Washington erupted so violently that it lost over 1,300 feet of elevation and the entire inside of the mountain fell down the face of the mountain, depositing the sediment in the valley below. Trees for miles north of the mountain were leveled and burned. The beauty of the mountain and lake below was altered forever. However, the event that would ultimately challenge the slow gradual change model of the Grand Canyon did not occur until two years later when, in the winter of 1982, another eruption occurred. At that time, due to the accumulation of snow on the mountain, when the eruption occurred, the massive amount of snow almost instantly turned into water and began rushing down the mountain. The huge surge of water carved a canyon one-quarter the size of the Grand Canyon.

The Canyon Formed Quickly

Picture 14 Rapid Erosion (photograph by Douglas Hamp).

What is so astounding, however, is that the canyon took only several hours to a few days to be formed. The power of the water quickly cut through the sediment that had been laid down two years prior in the first eruption (an event that occurred over a period of a few hours.) The walls of this mini Grand Canyon exposed almost identical stratification as found in the Grand Canyon. If both the strata from the deposition of the sediment and the deep cutting of a canyon (even through solid rock) can be formed in as little as a few hours, then how do we know that the stratification of the Grand Canyon is not also the product of massive sediment depositions left behind from a worldwide flood and the cutting of the canyon is not also an enormous release of water which happened shortly after? Austin notes:

> The small creeks which flow through the headwaters
> of the Toutle River today might seem, by present

appearances, to have carved these canyons very slowly over a long time period, except for the fact that the erosion was observed to have occurred rapidly! (Austin 1986: 3).

Footprints in the Ash

Drs. John Morris and Steven Austin book, *Footprints in the Ash*, deals at length with the overwhelming evidence. The book shows that formation of the Grand Canyon could have occurred quickly as a result of a worldwide flood rather than over millions of years just as things happened quickly on a smaller scale at Mount St. Helens. The evidence of Mount St. Helens provides a better and more consistent model of the age of the earth as being young, which, as we have seen, is the only acceptable conclusion one may come to from reading the Scriptures.

The Testimony of the Fossil Record

One final area to consider is the fossil record because it is considered to be proof positive of an old earth and the transitional forms needed to support the model of molecule-to-man evolution. Just as the traditional interpretation of stratification at the Grand Canyon, which indicates millions of years of age, is not necessarily the best interpretation of the data when compared with the Little Grand Canyon at Mount St. Helens, which happened very quickly, so too the traditional interpretation of the geological column as representing millions of years is to be questioned.

The geological column is the supposed order of evolutionary life-forms as recorded in the fossils found in sedimentary rocks. James Hutton in *Theory of the Earth* (1795) and Charles Lyell in *Principles of Geology* (1830) popularized the idea that the earth was hundreds of thousands and perhaps millions of years old based on the study of sedimentary rocks. As fossils were found in those rocks, the fossils were claimed to have a similar age to the rocks.

The geological column was a major source of inspiration and basis for Charles Darwin in the development of his evolutionary hypothesis. Though no "missing links" had been found in his day, he remained hopeful that the fossil record would eventually yield the intermediary fossils so badly needed to support his model. Nevertheless, he notes the conspicuous lack of evidence for his model:

> The number of intermediate varieties which have formerly existed on earth must be truly enormous. Why then is not every geological formation and every stratum full of such intermediate links? **Geology assuredly does not reveal any such finely graduated organic chain; and this, perhaps, is the most obvious and gravest objection which can be urged against my theory"** (Darwin 1902 edition, emphasis mine).

About 150 years have passed from when Darwin penned that statement, and unquestionably, millions of fossils have been found, but none of them are the "missing links" needed to substantiate his ideas. This is not only according to young-earth arguments (consistent with six literal days of creation), but also according to numerous evolutionists.

The geological column, drawn in detailed tables in text books, is the basis of the dating of the evolutionary stages. Ironically, this column, which is at the heart of the evolutionary timescale, is merely a construct, a mental abstraction (*Encyclopedia Britannica* 1985: 779). Derek Ager, past president of the British Geological Association, notes: "Nowhere in the world is the record, or even part of it, anywhere near complete" (Ager 1993: 14).

The geological column is the primary way by which fossils and rocks are dated. When a fossil is found, the rocks around it are checked to determine the age of the fossil; and vice versa, when a particular rock is found, it is compared to the surrounding fossils to determine its age. This type of circular reasoning is noted by several evolutionists.

J. E. O'Rourke, in the *American Journal of Science*, states: "The rocks do date the fossils, but the fossils date the rocks more accurately" (O'Rourke, Volume 276: 51). R. H. Rastal of Cambridge plainly acknowledges, "It cannot be denied that from a strictly philosophical standpoint geologists are here arguing in a circle." He then further defines what he means by circularity: "The succession of organisms has been determined by a study of their remains embedded in the rocks, and the relative ages of the rocks are determined by the organisms that they contain" (*Encyclopedia Britannica* 1976: 168).

Another evolutionist, Tom Kemp of Oxford, also is aware of the circular reasoning involved in the dating of the geological column. He states, "A circular argument arises: Interpret the fossil record in the terms of a particular theory of evolution, inspect the interpretation, and note that it confirms the theory" (Kemp 1985: 67).

D. B. Kitts of the University of Oklahoma stated regarding the circular foundation of the geological column in *Evolution*, Volume 28: "But the danger of circularity is still present. The temporal ordering of biological events beyond the local section may critically involve paleontological correlation [the geological column]" (Kitts 1974: 466). Kitts goes on to say "for almost all contemporary paleontologists it [the geological column] rests upon the acceptance of the evolutionary hypothesis" (ibid).

Many more evolutionists have made similar statements that are beyond the scope of this chapter to cover. Nevertheless, notice that accepting the geological column rests on the acceptance of evolution; and in turn, evolution is confirmed by the geological column. All of the evolutionists here agree that using the rocks to date the fossils and also using the fossils to date the rocks is circular reasoning. If one of the keystones upon which the supposed millions and billions of years of evolution is built is faulty (due to the fallacy of circular reasoning), then the fossil record is not a valid objection to a literal six-day creation.

Six Days Are Enough

We asked whether six days were enough for all the events of creation to occur in light of perhaps the greatest objections to a literal, six-day creation. Though we only scratched the surface of enormous areas of study, we did see that there are excellent answers available. It is possible from a physics' standpoint for the earth to be young and for the light from the edge of the universe fifteen billion light years away to have arrived in the span of six earth days. Likewise, the study of polonium "radiohalos" and zircon crystals provides weighty evidence that traditional methods of dating the rocks of the earth may be faulty. The data actually seem to confirm an earth of approximately six thousand years.

We also saw that when the Grand Canyon is compared to the Little Grand Canyon at Mount St. Helens, Washington, which is known to have formed rapidly, then millions of years are not required. In fact, the evidence points to the Grand Canyon having formed quickly from a cataclysmic event, such as a cataclysmic flood. Lastly, we saw that, according to evolutionists, the way in which fossils and rocks are dated is by circular reasoning. While these may not be the ultimate solutions to the four big "scientific" objections to a literal, six-day creation, they do sufficiently demonstrate that excellent answers exist. Thus we can affirm that the Bible is reliable in all that it records, especially regarding creation.

12 -In Six Days

Having looked in depth at a large amount of evidence concerning the first six days of creation, we are now ready to conclusively affirm that the first six days were literal days. To suggest that those days were figurative days in which billions of years passed flies in the face of the Bible, ancient commentators, and good science.

The basis of our study was whether the Bible is talking about six literal days or six day-ages. However, before we could adequately ask the question of what the Bible says, we had to ask ourselves what our method of interpretation would be because, after all, we didn't want to force anything upon the text of Scripture, but rather wanted to let it speak to us. The normal method as employed by the writers of the Bible was to accept God's Word literally. That is what Moses did, as well as Isaiah, Daniel, the Chronicler, and others.

With our method of interpretation in place, we examined both the literary style and also the testimony of experts in field of biblical literary criticism (most of whom are not Bible literalists) and found that it is not possible to claim that the Genesis creation account is merely a metaphor of a higher truth, nor is it figurative or allegorical. The question of prose or poetry played no part because both can be used to describe historical events.

Looking specifically at the use of *days* in Scripture, we concluded that, whenever a number is placed before either, it always refers to a definite period of time. This is consistent with what the ancient interpreters believed. In fact, Dr. Hugh Ross and others quoting him claimed that many of the ancient Jewish interpreters and early Church Fathers believed that *days* were long periods of time. What we saw, in the Jewish interpreters' and early Church Fathers' own words, was that every one of them (with the exception of Origen who taught that Jesus was a created being) believed that the days of creation were literal days. Church Father Victorinus of the fourth century even went so far as to tell us specifically that it was 24 hours. They just didn't believe in long periods of time. To clarify their words even more, they told us that they believed the earth was less than six thousand years old. The obvious implication of a world that is less than six thousand years old is that the days of creation could not have been long ages encompassing billions of years.

Even the tricky problem of how the dinosaurs fit into the confines of the Bible had an answer. The Bible speaks about the existence of dinosaurs, although by different names, as contemporaneous with man. As we saw, the Ica Stones fully support the written testimony of the Bible with what might be called "rock-solid" evidence. The approximately fifteen thousand stones have been proven to be authentic. They present a very serious challenge to the predominant evolutionary model.

Finally, we briefly considered a few of the "big problems" facing a belief in a literal, six-day creation and a young earth. Though certainly much more could be said, we at least saw that there exist extremely plausible solutions to the toughest challenges put forth. The examples were given merely to show that the evidence is out there, if one is willing to look.

We therefore affirm the simple reading of Genesis and other passages studied: God created in six literal days. Biblical creationism does not allow for God using Darwinian evolution as proposed by Progressive Creationism and Theistic Evolution nor does it warrant time anywhere in Scripture for the Gap Theory. Six literal days were more than enough time for Almighty God to create everything in the sea, on the earth and in the skies above.

Hopefully it is now apparent to the reader that the emperor has no clothes. The arguments of evolution have been so pervasive for such a long time that many Christians have capitulated to the pressure and have compromised the Bible. Rather than interpreting the world through the lens of the Bible, they have believed that man's "scientific" conclusions about the origin of the universe are more accurate than the testimony of Scripture. As a result, they now interpret the Bible through the lens of "science."

I hope that this examination of the evidence surrounding the question of the first six days has helped the reader to see that the compromising theories of Theistic Evolution, the Gap Theory, and Progressive Creationism are not biblically, linguistically, or historically valid interpretations of Scripture; nor are they necessary from the evidence that is out there. God's Word is accurate and true in every area of truth and is worthy of our trust.

Epilogue: Knowing the Creator

Perhaps you have seen from reading this book that there is no need to compromise the Bible with the evolutionary model. I think that even Darwin would be happy that the two are no longer confused in your mind! Let me now encourage you that God's Word, the Bible, is accurate, true, and trustworthy in all that it says. If you are already a Christian, then be encouraged that God loves you, and He rejoices in your resolve to believe His Word to the fullest. He has many wonderful promises in store for you that are written in the pages of the Bible.

If you have come to the conclusion that God's Word is faithful and accurate in all that it says but are not a Christian, then I would like to invite you to enter into a relationship with the God who created everything. God is awesome and mighty—just imagine how He made everything in only six days! Nevertheless, even more amazing is that He paid for our sins in less than one day! Jesus paid the price that our original parents, Adam and Eve, brought upon the world through their disobedience. But He also paid for your and my personal sin. Put your trust in Him now and receive a new life. You can trust the Word that He speaks to you:

> For the love of Christ compels us, because we judge thus: **that if One died for all, then all died;** and He died for all, that those who live should live no longer for themselves, but for Him who died for them and rose again [...] **Therefore, if anyone is in Christ, he is a new creation; old things have passed away; behold, all things have become new.** Now all things are of God, who has reconciled us to Himself through Jesus Christ, and has given us the ministry of reconciliation, that is, that God was in Christ reconciling the world to Himself, not imputing their trespasses to them, and

has committed to us the word of reconciliation. Now then, we are ambassadors for Christ, as though God were pleading through us: **we implore you on Christ's behalf, be reconciled to God**. For He made Him who knew no sin to be sin for us, that we might become the righteousness of God in Him (2 Corinthians 5:14–21, emphasis mine).

Jesus Himself also invites you to believe in Him: "Jesus said to her, 'I am the resurrection and the life. He who believes in Me, though he may die, he shall live. And whoever lives and believes in Me shall never die. Do you believe this?'" (John 11:25–26).

If you believe that Jesus died for your sins, as the Scriptures clearly say, then you can have eternal life. I invite you to receive His gift of life to you and then to rest in the promise that you are a new creation and will live forever with Christ.

Appendix 1:
Recommended Resources

The goal of this book was to show that biblically and historically creation took place in six literal days. I did not attempt to argue the finer points of creation science because I am not a specialist in those areas. However, there are many who are specialists in their respective fields who have spent many years developing plausible answers to the questions surrounding creation. I have listed the resources below that I believe will be of particular interest as you desire to dig deeper and discover that the science of creationists is just as good, and many times better, than that of the evolutionists. Visit www.thefirstsixdays.com for more recommendations.

Books

1. *Bones of Contention*, Marvin L. Lubenow
2. *Buried Alive*, Jack Cuozzo
3. *Darwin on Trial*, Phillip E. Johnson
4. *Darwin's Black Box*, Michael J. Behe
5. *Footprints in the Ash*, John Morris & Steven A. Austin
6. *In the Beginning*, Walt Brown
7. *Secrets of the Ica Stones*, Dennis Swift
8. *Starlight and Time*, D. Russell Humphreys
9. *Thousands Not Billions*, Dr. Don DeYoung
10. *What Darwin Didn't Know*, Geoffery Simmons
11. *The NEW Answers Book*, Ken Ham, general editor

DVDs

1. *A Question of Origins*, Eternal Productions
2. *Dinosaurs and Creation*, Mace Baker
3. *Dr. Jason Lisle Series*, Dr. Jason Lisle
4. *Dr. Terry Mortenson Series*, Dr. Terry Mortenson
5. *Scientific Evidence for Noah's Flood*, Mace Baker
6. *Incredible Creatures that Defy Evolution* (three-part series), Exploration Films
7. *Mount St. Helens*, ICR
8. *Putting the Puzzle Pieces Together: Global Tectonics and the Flood*, Dr. John Baumgardner
9. *Thousands Not Billions*, ICR
10. *The Privileged Planet*, Illustra Media
11. *Unlocking the Mystery of Life*, Illustra Media
12. *Where Does the Evidence Lead?* Illustra Media

Websites

www.answersingenesis.org

www.bible.ca

www.christiananswers.net

www.creationscience.com

www.icr.org

www.darwinisdead.com

Appendix 2:
Verses Containing
Numbers and Literal Days

Verses which contain the phrase "one day"

Gen 27:45, Gen 33:13, Num 11:19, 1Sam 2:34, 1Sam 14:1, 1Kgs 4:22, 1Kgs 20:29, 2Kgs 4:8, 2Kgs 4:11, 2Kgs 4:18, 2Chr 28:6, Esth 3:13, Esth 8:12, Isa 9:14, Isa 10:17, Isa 47:9, Isa 66:8, Zech 3:9, Zech 14:7

Verses which contain the phrase "two days"

Exod 16:29, Num 9:22, Num 11:19, 2 Sam 1:1, Ezra 10:13, Neh 6:15, Esth 9:27, Hos 6:2

Verses which contain the phrase "three days"

Gen 30:36, Gen 40:12, Gen 40:13, Gen 40:18, Gen 40:19, Gen 42:17, Exod 3:18, Exod 5:3, Exod 8:27, Exod 10:22, Exod 10:23, Exod 15:22, Num 10:33, Num 33:8, Josh 1:11, Josh 2:16, Josh 2:22, Josh 3:2, Josh 9:16, Judg 14:14, Judg 19:4, 1Sam 9:20, 1Sam 20:19, 1Sam 21:5, 1Sam 30:12, 1Sam 30:13, 2Sam 20:4, 2Sam 24:13, 1Kgs 12:5, 2Kgs 2:17, 1Chr 12:39, 1Chr 21:12, 2Chr 10:5, 2Chr 20:25, Ezra 8:15, Ezra 8:32, Ezra 10:8, Ezra 10:9, Neh 2:11, Esth 4:16, Amos 4:4, Jonah 1:17

Verses which contain the phrase "four days"

Judg 11:40

Verses which contain the phrase "five days"

Num 11:19

Verses which contain the phrase "six days"

Exod 16:26, Exod 20:9, Exod 20:11, Exod 23:12, Exod 24:16, Exod 31:15, Exod 31:17, Exod 34:21, Exod 35:2, Lev 23:3, Deut 5:13, Deut 16:8, Josh 6:3, Josh 6:14

Verses which contain the phrase "seven days"

Gen 7:10, Gen 8:10, Gen 8:12, Gen 31:23, Gen 50:10, Exod 7:25, Exod 12:15, Exod 12:19, Exod 13:6, Exod 13:7, Exod 22:30, Exod 23:15, Exod 29:30, Exod 29:35, Exod 29:37, Exod 34:18, Lev 8:33, Lev 8:35, Lev 12:2, Lev 13:4, Lev 13:5, Lev 13:21, Lev 13:26, Lev 13:31, Lev 13:33, Lev 13:50, Lev 13:54, Lev 14:8, Lev 14:38, Lev 15:13, Lev 15:19, Lev 15:24, Lev 15:28, Lev 22:27, Lev 23:6, Lev 23:8, Lev 23:34, Lev 23:36, Lev 23:39, Lev 23:40, Lev 23:41, Lev 23:42, Num 12:14, Num 12:15, Num 19:11, Num 19:14, Num 19:16, Num 28:17, Num 28:24, Num 29:12, Num 31:19, Deut 6:3, Deut 16:4, Deut 16:13, Deut 16:15, Judg 14:12, Judg 14:17, 1Sam 10:8, 1Sam 11:3, 1Sam 13:8, 1Sam 31:13, 1Kgs 8:65, 1Kgs 16:15, 1Kgs 20:29, 2Kgs 3:9, 1Chr 9:25, 1Chr 10:12, 2Chr 7:8, 2Chr 7:9, 2Chr 30:21, 2Chr 30:22, 2Chr 30:23, 2Chr 35:17, Ezra 6:22, Neh 8:18, Esth 1:5, Job 2:13, Ezek 3:15, Ezek 3:16, Ezek 43:25, Ezek 43:26, Ezek 44:26, Ezek 45:21, Ezek 45:23, Ezek 45:25

Appendix 3:
The Order of
Creation Versus Evolution

The differences in the order of appearance between the biblical creation account and evolution are not insignificant and are another reason why creation and evolution are incompatible. Furthermore, they serve to show that a literal reading of Genesis does not allow for theistic evolution. This list is taken from Dr. John D. Morris' 1994 book *The Young Earth:*

Biblical Order of Appearance	Evolutionary Order of Appearance
1. Matter created by God in the beginning	1. Matter existed in the beginning
2. Earth before the sun and stars	2. Sun and stars before the earth
3. Oceans before the land	3. Land before the oceans
4. Light before the sun	4. Sun, earth's first light
5. Atmosphere between two water layers	5. Atmosphere above a water layer
6. Land plants, first life-forms created	6. Marine organisms, first forms of life
7. Fruit trees before fish	7. Fish before fruit trees
8. Fish before insects	8. Insects before fish
9. Land vegetation before sun	9. Sun before land plants
10. Marine mammals before land mammals	10. Land mammals before marine mammals
11. Birds before land reptiles	11. Reptiles before birds
12. Man, the cause of death	12. Death, necessary antecedent of man

Bibliography

Ager, Derek (1993). *The New Catastrophism*. New York: Cambridge University Press.

Anthes, Emily (2006). *The Human-Influenced Evolution of Dogs*. Retrieved November 5, 2006, from www.seedmagazine.com/news/2006/07/the_humaninfluenced_evolution.php

Aquinas, Thomas (1947). *The Summa Theologica*. Benziger Bros. edition, Translated by Fathers of the English Dominican Province. Retrieved December 3, 2006, from www.ccel.org/a/aquinas/summa/FP/FP068.html

Archer, Gleason (1982). *Encyclopedia of Bible Difficulties*. Grand Rapids: Zondervan.

Augustine (1982). *The Literal Meaning of Genesis*. Translated and annotated by John Hammond Taylor, S. J., Volume 1. New York: Newman Press.

Austin, Steven (1984). *A Rapid Erosion at Mount St. Helens*.

Origins 11(2).:90–98. Retrieved October 6, 2006, from www.icr.org/research/index/researchp_sa_r04/

Austin, Steven. (1986). *Mt. St. Helens and Catastrophism* (#157). Retrieved September 27, 2006, from www.icr.org

Barr, James (1978). *Fundamentalism*. Philadelphia: Westminster Press.

Barr, James (April 23, 1984). *Letter to David C.C. Watson*: Oxford.

Basil. Catholic Information Network. Retrieved August 12, 2006, from www.cin.org/saints/basilgre.html

Batten, Don (1996). *Dogs Breeding Dogs?*

That's Not Evolution! Retrieved November 5, 2006, from www.answersingenesis.org/creation/v18/i2/dogs.asp

Behe, Michael J. (1996). *Darwin's Black Box*. New York: The Free Press.

Bermingham, Eric (2006). *Are the Ica Stones Authentic?* Retrieved August 11, 2006, from www.kolbecenter.org/bermingham_ica_authentic.html

Bleed, Peter (2000). *Digging out of the Scandal*. Retrieved September 24, 2006, from http://www.ancienteastasia.org/special/japanarchscandal2.htm

Bozarth, G. Richard. (Sept. 1979). "The Meaning of Evolution." *American Atheist Magazine*, 20.

Brown Driver Briggs (BDB), (1996). *Hebrew Lexicon*. Massachusetts: Hendrickson Publishers, (Reprint edition).

Buth, Randall (2005). *Living Biblical Hebrew, Introduction Part Two*, Mevasseret Zion: Biblical Language Center.

Buth, Randall (1994)."Methodological Collision Between Source Criticism and Discourse Analysis, The problem of 'Unmarked Temporal Overlay' and the pluperfect/nonsequential wayyiqtol" in Biblical Hebrew and Discourse Linguistics, ed. Robert Bergen, (S.I.L., 1994: 138–154).

Calvin, John *Institutes of the Christian Religion*. Retrieved July 21, 2006, from www.ccel.org/ccel/calvin/institutes.iv.iii.xxii.html

Catholic Encyclopedia "Constantine the Great." Retrieved July 19, 2006, from www.newadvent.org/cathen/04295c.htm

Cedars of Lebanon. Retrieved August 8, 2006, from www.mcforest.sailorsite.net/ListTest.html

Clergy Letter Project. Retrieved August 20, 2006, from www.butler.edu/clergyproject/religion_science_collaboration.htm

Collins English Dictionary (1992). New York: Harper Collins.

Collins, C. John (1995). *The Wayyiqtol As 'Pluperfect': When And Why* Pages 117–140 Tyndale Bulletin Vol.46.1 (May 1995).

Cuozzo, Jack (1998) *Buried Alive*. Green Forest, Arizona: Master Books.

Dalke, Kate (2002). *Who Is That Doggy In The Window? Scientists Trace The Origin Of Dogs*. Retrieved September 22, 2006, from www.genomenewsnetwork.org/articles/11_02/dog.shtml

Darwin, Charles (1902). *Origin of the Species*. London: John Murray.

Darwin, Francis ed. (1896). *Life and Letters of Charles Darwin Vol. 1, Chapter VIII*. Religion, Appleton Retrieved December 3, 2006, from www.darwiniana.org/religion.htm

Deem, Rich (2006a) *Is the Young-Earth Interpretation Biblically Sound?* Retrieved August 12, 2006, from www.godandscience.org/youngearth/youngearth.html

Deem, Rich, (2006b) *Millions of Years of Death and Suffering: Does the Old Earth View Compromise God's Character?* Retrieved 06/29/2006b www.godandscience.org/youngearth/longdays.html

Deem, Rich, (2006c) *Problems with a Young Earth Creation.* Retrieved 06/29/2006c www.godandscience.org/youngearth/longdays.html

DeYoung, Don (2005). *Thousands Not Billions.* Green Forest, Arizona: Master Books.

Doukhan, Jacques B. (1978). *The Genesis Creation Story: Its Literary Structure.* Andrews University Seminary Doctoral Dissertation Series, Berrien Springs, MI: Andrews University Press.

Duke, Charles (1854–55). *The Works of Philo. Complete and Unabridged.* Translated by Yonge, New Updated Edition Hedrickson (1993): (electronic version, The Word Bible Software).

Elert, Glenn ed, *The Physics Fact Book: Mass of an Elephant.* Retrieved August 9, 2006, from www.hypertextbook.com/facts/2003/EugeneShnayder.shtml

Early Church Fathers: Ante-Nicene Fathers, The Volumes 1—9 (1867). Edinburgh: (electronic version, The Word Bible Software).

Encyclopedia Britannica (1976 &1985). Chicago: Encyclopedia Britannica; Inc.

Etheridge J. W. transl. (1862) *Targum Pseudo-Jonathan and Onkelos to the Pentateuch*: (electronic version, The Word Bible Software).

Fields, Weston W. (1978). *Unformed and Unfilled.* Collinsville, Illinois: Burgener Enterprises.

Futuyma, Douglas J. (1986). *Evolutionary Biology.* Massachusetts: Sinauer Associates.

Gibson, J. C. L. (1977). *Canaanite Myths and Legends.* Edinburgh: T. & T. Clark.

Gillespie, Neal (1974). *Charles Darwin and the Problem of Creation.* Chicago, IL: The University of Chicago Press.

Gosline, Anna (2004) *Dinosaurs' 'Bulletproof' Armour*. Retrieved November 16, 2006, from www.NewScientist.com

Gould, Stephen (1990). *Natural History Magazine*. V 86.

Grigg, Russell (September 1993). *The Mind of God and The 'Big Bang'*. Creation, Volume 15, Issue 4.

Grigg, Russell (1997). *From The Beginning Of The Creation*. in Creation 19 (2):35–38 March 1997. Retrieved October 14, 2006, from answersingenesis.org/creation/v19/i2/beginning.asp

Harris, R. Laird, Gleason L. Archer Jr., & Bruse K. Waltke, (1980). *Theological Wordbook of the Old Testament*. Chicago: Moody Press.

Harris, Maurice H. Translator (1901). *Hebraic Literature Translations from the Talmud Midrashim and Kabbala*. Washington & London: M. Walter Dunne, Publisher.

Harrison, Jeffery, *Dinosaurs in the Bible*. Retrieved August 4, 2006, from www.totheends.com/dino.html

Humphreys, D. Russell (2004). *Starlight and Time*. Green Forest, Arizona: Master Books.

Hutton, James (1795). *Theory of the Earth*. Edinburgh (electronic version sacred-texts.com).

Indian Institute of Astrophysics. Retrieved August 9, 2006, from www.iiap.res.in/outreach/dinoext.html

Jackson, Wayne (2005). *Job, Behemoth, and Dinosaurs*. Publish date: Retrieved August 8, 2006, from ChristianCourier.com

Jacobs, Louis (1993). *In Quest of the African Dinosaur*. New York: Johns Hopkins.

Johnson, Phillip E. (1991). *Darwin on Trial*. Illinois: Intervarsity Press.

Josephus, *Antiquities of the Jews*. Translated William Whiston (electronic version, The Word Bible Software).

Josephus, *Wars of the Jews*. Translated William Whiston (electronic version, The Word Bible Software).

Joüon, P., & T. Muraoka (2005). *A Grammar of Biblical Hebrew*. Roma: Editrice Pontificio Istituto Biblico.

Kaiser, Walter C. (1970). *The Literary Form of Genesis 1–11, New Perspectives on the Old Testament*. ed. J. Barton Payne Waco, TX: Word Books.

Kautzsch, E. and A. E., Cowley, eds (1910). *Gesenius' Hebrew Grammar*, 2nd. ed. Oxford: Clarendon Press.

Keen, W. J. (1922). *I Believe in God and Evolution*. Philadelphia and London: J. B. Lippincott Company.

Keil & Delitzsch (1866). *Commentary on the Old Testament*. Eerdmans: Grand Rapids (1973 reprint).

Keith, Arthur (1872). *Introduction to the Everyman's Library edition of The Origin of Species*. Sixth Edition (1928 reprint). London: J. M. Dent & Sons.

Kemp, Tom (1985). *New Scientist. Volume 108, December 5.*

Kitts, D. B. (Sep. 1974) *Evolution. Volume 28.*

Koehler, Kenneth R. (1996). *Matter Waves*. Retrieved October 6, 2006, from www.rwc.uc.edu/koehler/biophys/9g.html

Lake, Kirsopp (1912). *The Apostolic Fathers*. (electronic version) Retrieved September 24, 2006, from http://www.ccel.org/ccel/richardson/fathers.vi.iii.ii.html

Leedy, Loreen and Street, Pat, *There's a Frog in My Throat*. New York, NY: Holiday House.

Liddel and Scott (1968). *Greek Lexicon*. Oxford: Claredon Press.

Lubenow, Marvin (2004). *Bones of Contention*. Oregon: Baker Books.

Lyell, Charles (1830). *Principles of Geology Volumes 1—3*. London: John Murray.

Matthews, L. H. (1971). *"Introduction" in: Darwin, Charles Origin of the Species*. London: J. M. Dent & Sons.

Moore, Edward *Origen of Alexandria* (185–254 AD). St. Elias School of Orthodox Theology. Retrieved July 19, 2006, from www.iep.utm.edu/o/origen.htm#SH3b

Morris, John and Steven Austin (2003). *Footprints in the Ash*. Green Forest, Arizona: Master Books.

Morris, John (1994) *The Young Earth*. Green Forest, Arizona: Master Books.

Nevins, John (1994). *The "Days" Of Creation In Genesis 1: Literal "Days" or Figurative "Periods/Epochs" Of Time?* Retrieved September 5, 2006, from *www.grisda.org/origins/21005.htm*

O'Connor, J. J. and E. F. Robertson (2000a). *MacTutor History of Mathematics* Retrieved October 21, 2006, from www.history.mcs.standrews.ac.uk/HistTopics/Babylonian_mathematics.htm

O'Connor, J. J. and E. F. Robertson (2000b). *MacTutor History of Mathematics* Retrieved October 21, 2006, from www.history.mcs.standrews.ac.uk/HistTopics/Babylonian_Pythagoras.html

Online Etymological Dictionary Entry: God. Retrieved August 2, 2006, from www.etymonline.com/index. php?search=god&searchmode=none

O'Rourke, J. E. *American Journal of Science*. Volume 276: 51.

Orr, James ed. (1913) *International Standard Bible Encyclopedia* (electronic version: The Word Bible Software).

Patton, Don R. (2006). *Art From Ancient Tombs In Peru*. Retrieved August 11, 2006, bible.ca/tracks/peru-tomb-art.htm#article

Peake, Tracey (2005). *NC State Scientist Finds Soft Tissue In T. Rex Bones*. Retrieved October 24, 2006, from www.eurekalert.org/pub_releases/2005-03/ncsu-nss032405.php

Pentecost, J. Dwight (1958). *Things to Come*. Grand Rapids, MI: Zondervan.

Pipa, Joseph A. Jr. *From Chaos to Cosmos: A Critique of the Framework Hypothesis*. Westminster Theological Seminary/California. (Draft January 13, 1998). Retrieved March 12, 2007, from http://capo.org/cpc/pipa.htm

Ramm, Bernard (1950). *Protestant Biblical Interpretation*. Grand Rapids, MI: Baker Books.

Random House Dictionary (electronic edition, 2006). Retrieved from www.randomhouse.com/

Rapaport, Samuel (1907). *Tales And Maxims From The Midrash*. London: George Routledge & Sons.

Raup, David M. (1979). *Conflicts between Darwin and Paleontology*. Field Museum of Natural History Bulletin, Vol. 50, No. 1.

Raup, David M. (1981). *New Scientist*. V. 90.

Redford, D. B. (1992). *Egypt, Canaan, and Israel in Ancient Times*. Princeton: Princeton University Press.

Research Communications Network, Breakthrough Report, (February 10, 1977). *"Mystery of the Radiohalos."* Interview with Robert Gentry, Retrieved October 28, 2006, from www.halos.com/reports/rcn-1977-mystery-of-the-radiohalos.htm

Roberts, A. & J. Donaldson, eds. (1885). *Translations of the Writings of the Fathers Down to AD 325.* Buffalo: The Christian Literature Publishing Company: (electronic version, The Word Bible Software).

Robertson, J. C. (1904). *Sketches of Church History from AD 33 to the Reformation.* New York: Edwin S. Gorham.

Ross, Hugh (1991). *The Fingerprint of God. 2nd ed.* Orange, CA: Promise Publishing.

Ross, Hugh (1994). *Creation and Time.* Colorado Springs, CO: Navpress.

Swift, Dennis (2004). *The Mystery of the Ica Stones: Did Man Walk with the Dinosaurs?* Retrieved October 4, 2006, from www.creationinfo. com/evcr/4_3_2004.htm

Swift, Dennis (2005). *Secrets of the Ica Stones and Nazca Lines.*

Swift, Dennis (2006). *The Dinosaur Figurines of Acambaro, Mexico.* Retrieved September 9, 2006, from www.bible.ca/tracks/tracks-acambaro.htm

Thompson, Keith Stewart (1991). *Living Fossil: The Story of the Coelacanth.* New York: Norton and Company.

Van Bebber, Mark and Paul S. Taylor, *Creation and Time: A Report on the Progressive Creationist Book by Hugh Ross.* Retrieved September 5, 2006, from www.christiananswers.net/catalog/bk-ct-ch1.html

Van Der Toorn, Karel Pieter and W Van Der Horst, Bob Becking (1999). *The Dictionary of Deities and Demons in the Bible.* Leiden: Brill.

Von Daniken, Erich (1999). *Chariots of the Gods.* Berkley: Berkley Trade, (Reprint edition).

Von Rad, Gerhard (1972). *Genesis: A Commentary.* Philadelphia: Westminster Press.

Webster, Noah (1828). *Dictionary of American English*: (electronic version, The Word Bible Software).

Wenham, Gordon J. (1987). *Genesis 1–15, Word Biblical Commentary, vol. 1.* Genesis. Waco, TX: Word Books.

Whitaker, R. E. (1972). *A Concordance of the Ugaritic Literature.* Massachusetts: Cambridge.

Wieland, Carl (2005). *Still Soft And Stretchy Dinosaur Soft Tissue Find— A Stunning Rebuttal of "Millions of Years."* Retrieved October 10, 2006, from http://www.answersingenesis.org/docs2005/0325Dino_tissue.asp

Yahuda, A. S. (1933). *The Language of the Pentateuch in its Relation to Egyptian.* London: Oxford University Press.

Yamada, Shoh (2002). *Politics and Personality: Japan's Worst Archaeology Scandal Volume VI, No. 3. Summer.* Retrieved September 05, 2006, from www.asiaquarterly.com/content/view/124/40/

Young, Davis A. (1988). *The Contemporary Relevance Of Augustine's View of Creation.* From The American Scientific Affiliation: Perspectives on Science and Christian Faith 40.1:42–45 (3/1988). Retrieved October 9, 2006, from www.asa3.org/ASA/topics/Bible-Science/PSCF3-88Young.html

Zorn, Joshua (1997). *The Testimony of a Formerly Young Earth Missionary.* American Scientific Affiliation. Retrieved May 07, 2006, from www.asa3.org/ASA/resources/zorn.html

Notes

¹ The Clergy Letter Project 2004.

2   Dr. Stan Sholar notes, "There are some hybrid concepts of this dichotomy here where God created things as a big bang but it evolved within the six-day framework and satisfied the literal words in the Bible more or less. This sort of manipulation of time and physics is a necessary part of the current big bang hypothesis also as they have had to impose an expansionary period where things happened faster than the speed of light, leading either to breaking Einstein's hypothesis, or else there was a growth of space which made the time seem to be superluminal when it actually was not. There are always those who say that big bang supports Genesis as a creation from nothing, since even the original dot could have been created" (Dr. Sholar, personal communication, September 21, 2006).

3   Some would even suggest that the dot was in fact nothing—and that nothing exploded into something.

4   In the twentieth century, the first version of the 'big bang' as the explosion of a 'primeval atom' was put forward by Abbé Georges-Henri Lemaître in 1931. Lemaître postulated that the universe originated as a single particle of vast energy but with near-zero radius (Grigg 1993).

5   I believe the Bible is a faithful and reliable historical document inspired by God. There are numerous excellent books and websites on the subject, which demonstrate the accuracy of the Bible. Visit christiananswers.net for general questions and answersingenesis.com for answers to many Bible and science questions.

6   "And I will put enmity between thee and the woman, and between the seed of thy son, and the seed of her sons … Nevertheless for them there shall be a medicine, but for thee there

will be no medicine; and they shall make a remedy for the heel in the days of the King Meshiha [Messiah]" (Targum Jonathan, Genesis 3:15).

[7]   See: http://www.tufts.edu/as/wright_center/cosmic_evolution/docs/splash.html.

[8]   A more predominant Progressive Creationist view is that God created the animals as we see them today (i.e. fixity of species) and they lived and died out over millions or billions of years. However, proponents of this view, such as Hugh Ross, do not believe in molecules-to-man evolution, but they do accept the evolutionary timescale for the geologic and fossil records (Dave Wright, Answers In Genesis staff, personal communication, June 9, 2007).

[9]   O'Connor and Robertson state concerning the Babylonians mathematical abilities, "Perhaps the most amazing aspect of the Babylonian's calculating skills was their construction of tables to aid calculation. Two tablets found at Senkerah on the Euphrates in 1854 date from 2000 BC. They give squares of the numbers up to 59 and cubes of the numbers up to 32 ..." (O'Connor and Robertson 2000a).

[10]   "Late 1800s. Dr. Matthew Maury is considered one of the major founders of the science of oceanography. He was also a creationist who believed in the absolute authority and accuracy of the Bible. One day while he was sick in bed, he asked his son to read the Bible to him. One of the verses his son read was Psalm 8:8. That particular verse mentioned paths in the seas. Believing that the Bible must be correct about these paths, he set out to find them. As a result, Dr. Maury was the first to discover (in modern times) that the seas were circulating systems with interaction between wind and water." *Scientific Foreknowledge in the Bible* retrieved from creationists.org/foreknowledge.html, October 22, 2006.

[11]   Quoted in N. C. Gillespie, Charles Darwin and the Problem of Creation (1979) p. 2 (University of Chicago book). See nwcreation.net/evolutionism.html, retrieved October 2, 2006.

[12] See Introduction pages: x, xi.

[13] The Targumim, cf. John Gill Commentary on 1 Cor 10:4 speak of the belief that the rock physically traveled with the Israelites: "that it again ascended with them to the highest mountains, and from the highest mountains it descended with them to the hills, and encompassed the whole camp of Israel, and gave drink to everyone at the gate of his own dwelling place; and from the high mountains it descended with them into the deep valleys" (Targum of Jonathan ben Uzziel).

[14] See: Leedy, Loreen and Street, Pat, *There's a Frog in My Throat.*

[15] The selected verses in Genesis 1 and in Numbers 29 are identical with the exception of the definite article ה (*he—the*). Genesis 1: יום שני (*yom sheni*). Numbers 29: יום השני (*yom hasheni*).

[16] *International Standard Bible Encyclopedia* "World."

[17] This is not to overlook the speculation that there may be parallel universes. However, by definition the word universe should encompass all that exists in the dimension of time and space.

[18] For further discussion see: Weston W. Fields (1976), *Unformed and Unfilled*, p. 58.

[19] For a further discussion on the copulative clause see: Kautzsch and Cowley, *Gesenius' Hebrew Grammar*, p. 484, section 154a, footnote 1.

[20] Joüon, P., & T. Muraoka, (2003; 2005: electronic version, Logos Software) note the use of the copulative clause (also known as the *vav explicativum*):

> On the other hand, a nominal or verbal clause with Waw forms a sort of parenthesis and precedes the main clause as in Gn 13.2 ואברהם כבד מאד *now Abraham was very rich* … ; 24.16 *now the young girl was very beautiful* …; Jon 3.3 *now Nineveh was an enormous city*; Gn 48.10 ועיני ישראל כבדו מזקן *now the eyes of Israel were heavy because of old age*; Josh 4.10 "*whilst the priests … stood* (עמדים) *in*

the middle of the Jordan ... the people hurriedly crossed over (וימהרו העם ויעברו)." This same type of clause is also found used in an independent fashion: 1Kg 1.1 (at the very beginning of a narrative) *now King David was old, advanced in age*; Gn 37.3 *now Israel loved Joseph more than all his sons.*

[21] "In almost all primitive creation stories in Egypt, the eternal substance that existed in the beginning and whose origin is not explained is water, the primeval ocean, Nun" (Redford 1992: 398).

[22] See Humphreys 2000: Appendix C, section 15 for a detailed, mathematical explanation of the physics involved.

He also notes that he based "a theory about the origin of the planetary magnetic fields on the possibility that the earth and other bodies in the solar system were originally created as pure water" (Humphreys 2004: 73). He remarks that his theory has been extremely successful in predicting measurements of the magnetic fields of Uranus and Neptune.

[23] The word is in the Pa'al form in Jeremiah 23:9.

[24] Keil & Delitzsch confirm this "The creative Spirit of God, the principle of all life (Psalm 33:6; Psalm 104:30), which worked upon the formless, lifeless mass, separating, quickening, and preparing the living forms, which were called into being by the creative words that followed. רחף in the *Piel* is applied to the hovering and brooding of a bird over its young, to warm them, and develop their vital powers (Deuteronomy 32:11). In such a way as this the Spirit of God moved upon the deep, which had received at its creation the germs of all life, to fill them with vital energy by His breath of life" (K&D 1866 Genesis 1:2).

[25] Dr. Randall Buth notes "in telling stories, the past tense is used with a special word order to grammatically signal events as a break in the flow of the story. It marks a discontinuity. That is, something is put in front of the verb [...] This is done when the author wants to break the time flow of the story, or when the author wants to mark a boundary of unity [...]" (Buth 2005: 52).

There could be no better way to indicate that Genesis 1:1 is an absolutely new and dramatic event than by using the simple past tense (also commonly referred to as the perfect or *qatal* tense).

26 This is commonly known in Hebrew grammar as the *vayyiqtol* tense.

27 Numbers chapter 28 verses 3 and 4 show that a literal day was comprised of *morning* and *evening*. "This is the offering made by fire which you shall offer to the LORD: [...] day by day (ליום), as a regular burnt offering. The one lamb you shall offer in **the morning**, the other lamb you shall offer in **the evening** [...]" (Numbers 28:3–4, emphasis mine).

28 Interestingly Deuteronomy 19:15 says that "by the mouth of two or three witnesses the matter shall be established." Perhaps God has repeated Himself to assure us of the certainty of the statement.

29 "Followed by an inf. c., בְּ, forms a periphrasis for the gerund, though in English it is commonly to be rendered by a verb and conj., viz.: 1. as a *temporal* conj., as בהבראם, *in their being created* = *when* they *were* created" BDB. "This use of the infinitive construct is especially frequent in connection with *be* or *ke* to express time-determinations (in English resolved into a temporal clause" Gesenius' (1910).

30 Thanks to Dr. Bill Gallagher for helping me word that correctly (personal communication October 20, 2006).

31 According to BDB, the word *toledoth* means: 1) descendants, results, proceedings, generations, genealogies; 1a) account of men and their descendants; 1a1) genealogical list of one's descendants; 1a2) one's contemporaries; 1a3) course of history (of creation, etc.); 1b) begetting or account of heaven (metaphorically).

32 There has been considerable discussion concerning this particular form of the *wayyiqtol* as past perfect (pluperfect). Some have skillfully argued that this form of the verb cannot be translated with the pluperfect (see Buth: 1994). Others, such as

C. John Collins make a strong case in favor of the *wayyiqtol* as a pluperfect. In his article, *The Wayyiqtol As 'Pluperfect': When And Why* (1995), he examines the possibility that the *wayyiqtol* verb form, without a previous perfect, may denote a pluperfect tense. He concludes that there is an unmarked pluperfect usage of the *wayyiqtol* verb form which is present in particular in Genesis 2:19. The position regarding the use of the *wayyiqtol*, pluperfect tense in Genesis 2:19 is held by many Bible commentators including the renowned Hebrew scholars Keil & Delitsch as well as John Gill. The possible use of the pluperfect is also given as an alternative translation in the ESV, NRS (parallel to verse 7). The NIV, on the other hand, translates *vayitzer* as "had formed."

[33] Dr. Joseph Pipa argued in a 1998 article "In Genesis 2:19, it communicates the idea of logically anterior circumstances. Waltke and O'Connor list pluperfect as a subvariety of epexegetical use. After interacting with Driver, they say, "Moreover, wayyqtl in the received text, the object of our grammatical investigation, must be understood to represent the pluperfect." They offer two examples of this usage from the Pentateuch (Num. 1:47–49; Exod. 4:11–12,18). Moses, in fact, uses the waw consecutive for logically anterior acts or as a pluperfect throughout Pentateuchal narrative. For example, in Exodus 11:1 Moses inserts a waw consecutive as a pluperfect into a sequential narrative in order to introduce a revelation previously given to Moses: "Now the Lord said to Moses, 'One more plague I will bring on Pharaoh and on Egypt ...'" This section begins with the waw consecutive, but Moses introduces it in the middle of his last interview with Pharaoh (Exodus 10:24–11:8). As such 11:1–3 serves as a backdrop, a flashback so-to-speak, for his message to Pharaoh. The NIV translates Exodus 11:1 in the same way as it does Gen. 2:19, "Now the Lord had said to Moses, ..." For the sake of emphasis, Moses would use the waw consecutive as a pluperfect and then resume the chronological sequence of his narrative."

[34] For a detailed explanation of the language of Israel in the first century, see Hamp (2005) *Discovering the Language of Jesus* Calvary Publishing, Santa Ana.

[35]   Also known as Pseudo Jonathan.

[36]   Before the discovery of the Dead Sea Scrolls, the sect known as the Essenes, which Josephus describes in detail in *Wars of the Jews* book 2, chapter 8, there was no record of it ever existing. Josephus' account has since been corroborated by much of the material finds at the Qumran compound near the Dead Sea as well as by the Scrolls themselves.

[37]   The Mishna deals with the Mosaic Law and applies it to every conceivable area of life.

[38]   This is signified by the term "space-time continuum." Dr. Sholar notes: "The space-time continuum, however, was a mathematical assumption of Einstein leading to relativity ... which has predicted outcomes of certain experiments with some degree of accuracy. However, there are many today who believe that time and space are not so intertwined that they must be cojoined as a continuum the way Einstein postulated. There are other theories that consider space and time quite distinctly separate, yet predict the same results as does relativity. Since most scientists are not experts in relativity, it is easier for them to accept the establishment's entrenchment of a theory into textbooks and academia, than to swim upstream against the more popular theory, with an alternative that gives similar answers, though void philosophical problems like paradoxes. The almost certain fact that space and time were each created anew does not depend upon whether or not they are connected as Einstein postulates, or are completely disparate and separate entities" (Dr. Stan Sholar, personal communication, September 21, 2006).

[39]   All of the early Church Fathers are cited from *The Early Church Fathers: Ante-Nicene Fathers* Volumes 1—9 (1867), Edinburgh, using the electronic version of The Word Bible Software, unless otherwise stated.

[40]   The belief of the ancient commentators that the entirety of human history would last six thousand years is not specifically stated in the Bible. Nevertheless, the belief clearly shows that

they believed the earth to be young and not millions or billions of years old.

[41] This was actually recorded by another ancient writer, Photius.

[42] Weston W. Fields, in his book *Unformed and Unfilled* (Presbyterian and Reformed Publishing Company, 1978), provides a thorough discussion of the Gap Theory and its fatal flaws. See also answersingenesis.org/creation/v3/i3/gap_theory.asp.

[43] For a discussion on the Gap Theory, see: Russell Grigg *From the Beginning of the Creation*, answersingenesis.org/creation/v19/i2/beginning.asp.

[44] A plethora of excellent research has been done in this area demonstrating conclusively that many of the supposed transitional forms were hoaxes, fanciful reconstructions based on pigs' teeth, merely extinct apes, or just humans—none of which is the missing evolutionary link between men and the imagined ancestor. Marvin Lubenow's *Bones of Contention* is a scholarly, yet very readable, creationist assessment of human fossils. Mr. Lubenow systematically demonstrates that the bones in question are not the transitional forms the paleontologists have been telling us for so many years.

[45] See Jeffrey Harrison's article *Dinosaurs and the Bible* (2006) for a detailed listing of over forty verses dealing either directly or indirectly with dinosaurs. www.totheends.com/dino.html.

[46] King James Concordance (electronic version: The Word Bible Software): KJV total number of occurrences (27) of the root תנים / תנין tannin / tannim: dragons 15–Deu 32:33, Job 30:29, Psa 44:19, Psa 74:13, Psa 148:7, Isa 13:22, Isa 34:13, Isa 35:7, Isa 43:20, Jer 9:11, Jer 10:22, Jer 14:6, Jer 49:33, Jer 51:37, Mic 1:8; dragon 6–Psa 91:13 (2), Isa 27:1, Isa 51:9, Jer 51:34, Eze 29:3; serpent 2–Exo 7:9–10; monsters 1–Lam 4:3; serpents 1–Exo 7:12; whale 1–Job 7:12; whales 1–Gen 1:21.

[47] Dave Wright notes "The sea creatures, like the plesiosaur, are not actually considered dinosaurs. The term "dinosaur" is used

to refer to those that live on land. Therefore, dinosaurs were land animals that were created on day six" (Dave Wright, Answers In Genesis staff, personal communication, June 9, 2007).

[48]   Dr. Sholar notes "when He says, 'Look now at the behemoth …' this speaks strongly to me of coexistence. If it was extinct, however, the 'look now' makes no sense for he would not have had any historical record of it" (Sholar, personal communication September 21, 2006).

[49]   *Cedars of Lebanon.* Retrieved August 8, 2006, from www.mcforest.sailorsite.net/ListTest.html.

[50]   Exodus 4:4, Deuteronomy 28:13, Deuteronomy 28:44, Judges 15:4, Isaiah 19:14–15.

[51]   KTU 1.5 I:1 27.

[52]   See: http://www.skepdic.com/icastones.html and http://www.csicop.org/si/2004-07/hoaxes.html.

[53]   The reader is encouraged to study Marvin Lubenow's *Bones of Contention* as mentioned earlier as well as Jack Cuozzo's *Buried Alive* (2003) to examine the evidence.

[54]   "Ancient Angkor was first published in Thailand in 1999 by River Books Ltd., Bangkok." Pg. 144. They also state: "The large, beautiful 320 page book, *Angkor, Cities and Temples*, by the same author and photographer, includes a half-page picture of the stegosaur sculpture." On page 213 the author describes it as "an animal which bears a striking resemblance to a stegosaurus." See bible.ca/tracks/dino-art.htm.

[55]   For detailed results on the dating of a rock of known age, see: answersingenesis.org/creation/v23/i3/radiodating.asp.

About the Author

Douglas Hamp earned his MA in the Hebrew Bible and the Ancient Near East from the Hebrew University of Jerusalem, Israel. During his three years in Israel, he studied both modern and biblical Hebrew, biblical Aramaic, Koine Greek, and other ancient languages as well as ancient texts and the archeology of the Bible. He is currently an assistant pastor at Calvary Chapel Costa Mesa, where he teaches at the School of Ministry and Graduate School.

Booking Information

To request a presentation of *The First Six Days* or *Discovering the Language of Jesus*, please visit:

www.thefirstsixdays.com

or

www.languageofjesus.com

Also by Douglas Hamp

Discovering the Language of Jesus

For the last 150 years, both popular and academic views have asserted that Jesus spoke Aramaic as His primary language of communication since supposedly Hebrew died out after the children of Israel were taken into Babylonian captivity. This view, however, is not based on the testimony of the Old Testament, the New Testament, historical sources, or Jesus' actual words. Just which language did Jesus and His disciples speak?

Pastor and teacher Douglas Hamp takes you on a journey through history, Scripture, and linguistics to solve the puzzle. By *Discovering the Language of Jesus*, you will gain a deeper understanding of Jesus' words and culture and will be fully convinced that every detail in God's Word is accurate, reliable, and worthy of your trust.

ISBN: 1597510173

www.languageofjesus.com